Mcewan's Easy Shorthand

McEWAN'S
EASY
SHORTHAND

A DICTIONARY

of

Twenty Thousand Outlines

Compiled and Prepared by

EVELYN BULLEYN

PRICE $1.50

The McEwan Shorthand Corporation
72 West Adams Street
Chicago

Copyright by
The McEwan Shorthand Corporation

1919

1114

PREFACE

By undertaking and completing this important addition to the literature of McEwan's Easy Shorthand, Miss Evelyn Bulleyn has placed me under an obligation that cannot well be expressed in words. To her it was indeed a labor of love—love for the art for its own sake. It may give her satisfaction to know that no other lady has ever accomplished such a task as the one she has so well performed.

It was once said of the compiler of a certain shorthand dictionary that he had inserted only the easy words that everybody could write, and had omitted all that ever gave students any trouble. That charge cannot be brought against the compiler of this work. The very large proportion of lengthy words that Miss Bulleyn has chosen is quite noticeable and, in consequence, the book cannot fail to be most helpful.

It often happens that more than one outline can be formed for the same word. Not infrequently both outlines are equally practical, and then it is merely a matter of choice and taste. A choice of practical outlines is frequently given in the following pages.

Since Miss Bulleyn completed this dictionary several important changes have been made in the system. For instance, the U-OO vowel may be used to express SOO before M and N. The old form for *accumulate* was written so that the U vowel was attached to M. According to the new rule it should be attached to K. But, as a matter of fact, in lengthy outlines it makes little difference whether the vowel be attached to the preceding or the following consonant.

It will be noticed that in the outline for *billowy* a short dash has been inserted. This is to indicate the vowel E (Y) with which the word ends. It is very seldom necessary to express both of two concurring vowels, but if necessary it may be done by using a light dot for A, a heavy dot for O, a light dash for E and a heavy dash for OO.

In a few cases Miss Bulleyn has given the most popular English pronunciation. For instance, in *enunciation* she has given the SH sound to C—very common among the educated classes in England. Any who prefer the American pronunciation—S— will express the sound by writing the A vowel on the wrong side of N.

Not a few of the outlines chosen are most ingenious. Evidently Miss Bulleyn saw the necessity for distinguishing between *fixature* and *fixture*. And she has done so by inserting the A circle inside the STR loop.

Many contractions are suggested for lengthy technical words.

The dictionary will be most useful to all students who intend to pursue the study of McEwan's Easy Shorthand beyond the knowledge and skill required for mere business correspondence.

Miss Bulleyn's original copy has been reduced by the engraver almost to half scale; therefore the characters in practice should be written larger than they appear in this work, the object of which is to show the form only.

This edition of the dictionary, like all such first issues, is more or less experimental. At a not very distant date a new edition will be issued. Indeed, Miss Bulleyn is engaged on that new edition already. When the new edition appears, enlarged and very much approved, it will be sold at half price to all who have purchased this edition, on condition that they return this book with their remittance.

OLIVER McEWAN.

A

aback
abandon
abandoned
abase
abasement
abash
abate
abated
abatement
abbess
abbey
abbot
abbreviate
abbreviated
abbreviation
abdicate
abdomen
abduction
aberration
abet
abettor
abhor
abhorrence
abide
abiding
abilities
ability
abject
abjure
able
able-bodied
ablution
abnormally
aboard
abolish
abolition
abominable
abomination
aboriginal
aborigines
abortive
abound
about
above
abreast
abridge
abridgment
abroad
abrogate

abrupt
abscess
abscond
absence
absent
absent-
   minded
absolute
absolutely
absolution
absolve
absorb
absorbingly
abstain
abstemious
abstemious-
   ness
abstinence
abstract
abstraction
abstruse
absurd
absurdity
abundance
abundant
abuse
abusive
abut
abutting
abyss
acacia
academical
academy
accede
accelerate
acceleration
accent
accentuate
accept
acceptable
acceptation
acceptance
access
accessible
accession
accessory
accident
accidentally
acclaim
acclamation

acclivity
accomodate
accomodation
accompaniment
accompany
accomplice
accomplish
accord
accordance
accordingly
accost
account
accountable
accountant
accountancy
accoutrements
accredit
accrue
accumulate
accumulation
accuracy
accurate
accurately
accurse
accursed
accusation
accuse
accustom
ace
acerbity
acetous
ache
achieve
achievement
acid
acidulate
acidulated
acidulous
acknowledge
acknowledged
acknowledg-
   ment
acorn
acoustics
acquaint
acquaintance
acquarium
acquiesce
acquire
acquisition

* See note in Preface.

acquit
acquitted
acquittal
acre
acreage
acrid
acrimon-
  ious
acrimony
acrobats
act
action
active
activity
actor
actress
actual
actualize
actually
actuate
acumen
acute
adage
adamant
adapt
adaptation
adapted
add
added
addendum
adder
addict
addicted
addition
additional
addle
address
adduce
adept
adequate
adhere
adhered
adherents
adhesion
adhesive
adieu
adit
adjacent
adjective
adjoin

adjourn
adjudge
adjudicate
adjunct
adjuration
adjust
adjusting
adjustment
admeasure-
  ment
administer
administrate
administra-
  tion
administra-
  tor
administra-
  trix
admirable
admiral
admirality
admiration
admire
admissible
admission
admit
admittance
admixture
admonish
admonition
ado
adopt
adopted
adoption
adolescent
adorable
adoration
adore
adorn
adrift
adroit
adroitness
adulation
adult
adulterate
adulteration
adultery
advance
advantage
advantageous

advent
adventure
adventurer
adventurous
adverb
adverbial
adversary
adverse
adversity
advert
advertise
advertisement
advertiser
advice
advisable
advise
advocate
advowson
aerial
aeroplane
afar
affable
affability
affair
affect
affectation
affected
affection
affectionate
affidavit
affinity
affirm
affirmation
affix
afflicting
affliction
affluence
affluent
afford
affray
affright
affront
afloat
afraid
after
aftermath
afternoon
afterwards
again
against

age
aged
agency
agent
aggrandize
aggravate
aggregate
aggression
aggressive
aggressor
aggrieve
agility
agitate
agitation
agnomen
agonize
agony
agree
agreement
agreeable
agricultural
agriculture
agricultur-
    ist
aground
ague
ahead
aid
aided
aider
ail
ailment
aim
aimless
aimlessly
air
air-gun
air-hole
airiness
airpump
airy
aitch
ajar
akin
alabaster
alacrity
a-la-mode
alarm
alas
albatross

album
alchemy
alcoves
alder
aldermen
ale
alehouse
alert
algebra
alias
alien
alienate
alienation
alight
alike
alimentary
alive
all
allay
allegation
allege
allegiance
allegory
alleviate
alley
alliance
alligators
allot
allow
allowable
allowance
allowed
allows
alloy
allude
allure
allurement
alluring
allusions
ally
almanac
almighty
almond
almost
alms-
    giving
almshouse
aloft
alone
along

alongside
aloof
already
also
altar
alteration
alternate
although
altitude
altogether
alum
always
amalgamate
amalgamation
amass
amateur
amaze
amazed
amazement
amazing
ambassador
amber
ambiguity
ambiguous
ambition
ambitious
amble
ambrosial
ambush
amelioration
amend
amendments
amenity
amiable
amicable
amid
amidst
amiss
amity
ammunition
amnesty
among
amongst
amorous
amount
ample
amplifica-
    tion
amplify
amputate

amputation	annoyance	aperture
amuse	annoyed	aphorism
amusement	annually	apiary
amusing	annuity	apiece
an	annul	apocalypse
anachron-ism	anodyne	apologetic
	annoint	apologize
analogous	annointed	apologized
analogy	anomalous	apology
analysis	anomaly	apoplexy
anarchism	another	apostacy
anarchist	answer	apostate
anarchy	answerable	apostle
anathema	ant	apostrophize
anatomy	antagonism	apothecary
ancestors	antagonist	apothegm
anchor	antecedent	appal
anchorage	antedate	appalment
anchovy	antelope	apparatus
ancient	anterior	apparel
anecdote	anthem	apparent
anew	anthill	apparently
angel	anticipate	apparition
angelic	anticipation	appeal
anger	antidote	appear
angle	antiquary	appearance
angry	antimony	appease
anguish	antipathy	appellation
angular	antipodes	append
animadversion	antique	appendage
animadvert	antiquity	appendix
animal	antiseptic	appertain
animate	antlers	appetency
animation	antonym	appetite
animosity	anvil	applaud
ankle	anxiety	applause
annals	anxious	apple
annex	anxiously	applicable
annexation	any	application
annihilate	anybody	applied
annihilation	anyhow	apply
anniversary	anyone	appoint
annotate	anything	appointment
annotation	anywhere	apportion
announce	apace	apposite
announced	apart	appreciate
announcing	apartment	appreciation
announce-ment	apathy	apprehend
	apes	apprehension
annoy	aperient	apprehensive

apprentice
apprentice-
    ship
apprise
approach
approbation
appropriate
appropria-
    tion
approval
approve
appriori
approximate
approxima-
    tion
appurten-
    ance
apricot
april
apron
a propos
apt
aptitude
aquatic
aqueous
arable
arbiter
arbitral
arbitrary
arbitrate
arbitration
arbor
arcade
arch
archaic
archaio-
    logy
archbishop
archery
archetype
architect
architecture
archives
archway
ardent
ardour
arduous
area
arena
argue

argument
arid
aright
arise
aristocracy
arithmetic
ark
arm
armament
armistice
armour
armoury
armpit
army
aroma
aromatic
around
arouse
arraign
arrange
array
arrears
arrest
arrested
arrival
arrive
arrogance
arrogant
arrogate
arrow
art
artery
artful
artichoke
article
articulate
articula-
    tion
artifice
artificial
artillery
artisan
artist
artless
as
asbestos
ascend
ascendant
ascension
ascent

ascertain
ascribe
ash
ashore
aside
ask
askance
aslant
asleep
asparagus
aspect
aspen
asperity
asperse
asphyxia
aspiration
ass
assail
assailant
assassinate
assault
assay
assemblage
assemble
assembling
assembly
assent
assert
assertain
assertion
assess
assets
asseverate
assiduity
assiduous
assign
assignation
assignee
assimilate
assist
assistant
assistance
assize
associate
association
assort
assortment
assuage
assume
assumption

assurance	attribution	avenge
assure	auburn	avenue
astern	auction	aver
asthma	auctioneer	average
asthmatic	audacious	averse
astonish	audacity	aversion
astonish-ment	audible	avert
astrakhan	audience	aviary
astray	auditor	avidity
astrology	augur	avocation
astronomer	aught	avoid
astute	augment	avouch
asunder	augmenta-tion	avow
asylum	august	avowal
at	aunt	await
ate	au revoir	awake
atheism	auricular	award
atheist	aurora borealis	awarded
athletic	auspices	aware
athwart	auspicious	away
atlas	austere	awe
atmosphere	austerity	awesome
atom	authentic	awful
atone	authenti-cate	awfully
atonement	authenticity	awkward
atrocious	author	awl
atrocity	authorita-tive	awning
attach	authority	awry
attachment	authorization	axe
attack	authorize	axle-tree
attain	autobiography	aye
attainment	autocracy	azure
attaint	autocratic	
attempt	autograph	Babble
attend	automatic	baboon
attendant	automaton	baby
attention	automobile	bachelor
attentive	autopsy	back
attenuate	autumn	backbite
attest	autumnal	backer
attestation	auxiliary	backslide
attic	avail	backward
attire	available	backwardness
attitude	avalanche	bacon
attorney	avarice	bacteriology
attract	avaricious	bad
attraction		bade
attractive		badge
attribute		badger
		badinage

badly
badness
baffle
bag
baggage
bagpipe
bail
bailiff
bait
bake
baker
balance
balcony
bald
bale
baleful
balk
balky
ball
ballad
ballast
ballet
balloon
ballot
balm
balsam
balsamic
baluster
bamboo
ban
banana
band
bandages
bandit
banditti
bandy
bane
baneful
bang
banish
banishment
banisters
banjo
bank
banker
banking-
    account
banking-
    house
bank-note

bankrupt
bankruptcy
banner
banquet
banter
baptism
baptize
bar
barb
barbarian
barbaric
barbarism
barbarous
barber
bard
bare
bare-foot
barely
bargain
bargaining
bargeman
baritone
bark
barky
barley
barley-
    sugar
barn
barn
barnacle
barograph
barometer
baron
baroness
baronet
barracks
barrel
barren
barricade
barriers
barrister
barrow
barter
base
basest
baseless
basement
bashful
basin
basis

bask
basket
bas-relief
bastard
baste
bastinado
bat
batable
bat-fowling
batch
bath
bathe
bathos
bath-room
batter
battered
battery
batting
battle
battle-field
battlement
battleship
battue
bauge
bawl
bay
bayonet
bay-window
bazaar
be
beach
beacon
bead
beadle
beagle
beak
beam
bear
bearable
bearing
beard
bearded
bearer
beast
beastly
beat
beaten
beatitude
beau
beau-ideal

beauteous
beautiful
beautify
beauty
beaver
becalm
because
bechance
beck
beckon
become
becoming *
bed
bedside
bedaub
bed-
    chamber
bed-clothes
bedew
bedridden
bedstead
bee
beech
beef
beef-tea
bee-hive
beele
been
beer
beet
beetle
beet-root
befall
befit
befitting
before
before-
    hand
befoul
beg
beget
beggar
beggary
begged
begin
beginner
beginning
begone
beguile
begun *

behalf
behave
behaviour
behead
behest
behind
behold
behoves
being
belabor
belated
belch
beleaguer
belfry
belie
belief
believe
believer
belighted
belittle
bell
belles-
    lettres
belliger-
    ent
bellow
belly
belong
belongings
beloved
below
belt
bench
benches
bencher
bend
beneath
benedic-
    tion
benefac-
    tion
benefactor
benefice
beneficence
beneficent
beneficial
benefit
benevolence
benevolent
benighted

benign
benignant
bent
benumb
bequeath
bequeathed
bequest
bequote
bereave
bereave-
    ment
berg
berme
berried
berry
berth
beryl
beseech
beseem
beseeming
beset
beside
besiege
beslime
besmear
besmirch
bespeak
best
bestial
bestir
bestow
bestowal
bestride
bet
betide
betimes
betoken
betray
betrayal
betroth
betrothal
betrothed
better
between
betwixt
beverage
bevy
bewail
beware
bewilder

* See Preface

bewilder-
  ment
bewitch
bewitching
beyond
bias
bib
bibber
bible
bicker
bickern
bicorn
bicycle
bicyclist
bid
bidder
bide
bier
bifold
big
bigot
bigotry
bike
bile
bilge
bilious
bilk
bill
billiards
billow
billowy
bin
binds
bindweed
binnacle
binocle
biography
biologi-
  cal
biology
biped
birch
birds
birth
birthday
birthplace
birth-
  right
biscuit
bisect

bishop
bit
bitch
bite
biting
bitter
bitter-
  ness
bitumen
bizarre
blab
black
blackberry
blackboard
blacken
blacker
blackguard
black-lead
blackmail
blackness
blackrust
blacksmith
bladder
blade
bladebone
blades
bladed
blain
blamable
blame
blameless
blanch
bland
blandish
blank
blanket
blankly
blanks
blaspheme
blasphemed
blasphe-
  mous
blasphemy
blast
blatter
blaze
blazer
blazon
bleach
bleak

bleakness
blear
bleat
bleed
blemish
blench-
blend
blending
blent
bless
blessed
blesséd
blessedness
blessing
blest
blew
blight
blind
blindness
blink
bliss
blissful
blister
blithe
blithesome
blizzard
bloat
block
blockade
blockhead
block-tin
blood
bloody
bloom
blossom
blot
blotch
blote
blouse
blow
blower
blowy
blubber
blue
bluff
blunder
blundering
blunt
bluntness
blur

blurt	bony	bottom
blush	booby	bouche
blushed	book	boudoir
blush-	book-	bough
ingly	keeping	bought
bluster	bookmaker	boulder
blustering	bookman	boultin
boar	book-post	bounce
board	bookseller	bounced
boarder	boom *	bound
boast	boomerang	boundary
boasting	boon	bounden
boaster	boor	boundless
boat	boorish	bounds
boatman	boot	bounteous
bode	booth	bountiful
bodeful	bootless	bounty
bodily	boots	bouquet
body	booty	bourne
bog	border	bout
boggle	borderer	bovine
boggy	bordering	bow (v)
bohea	border-	bow (n)
bohemian	land	howed (v)
boil	borderers	bowed (n)
boiler	bordure	bower
boiling	bore	bowery
boils	boredom	bowl
boisterous	boring	howler
bold	borne	bowless
boldness	borough	bowline
bole	borrow	howman
bolero	borrowed	bowse
bolster	bosa	bow-window
bolt	boscage	box
holted	bosh	boxer
bolting	bosom	box-wood
bolus	bosquet	boy
bomb	boss	boycott
bond	bossage	boyhood
bondage	botanic	boyish
bond-	botanical	brace
servant	botanist	brachiel
bone	botany	brachylogy
boned	botch	bracken
bonedust	bote	bracket
boneless	both	brackish
bonnet	bother	bract
bonny	bottle	brad
bonus	bottler	brag

see Preface

braggart	breathing	bringing
braid	breathing-	brink
brail	time	brisk
brain	breathless	brisket
brain-fever	breech	bristle
brainless	breed	brit
braise	breeder	brittle
brake	breeding	broach
bramble	breeze	broached
bran	bret	broad
branch	brethren	broadcast
branchiate	brevet	broaden
brand	brew	brocade
brandish	brewery	brocatel
brandy	bribe	brochure
brass	bribed	brook
brat	bribery	brogue
bravado	brick	broil
brave	bricklayers	broiling
bravery	brick-	broke
bravo	maker	broken-
brawl	brickwork	hearted
brawling	brickyard	broker
brawn	bridal	brokerage
brawny	bride	bromate
bray	bridges	bromatology
braze	bridle	bromide
brazen	bridle-path	bronchial
brazier	bridoon	bronze
brazil	brief	broods
breach	briefer	brooch
bread	briefly	broom
breadth	brier	broth
break	brig	brother
breakable	brigade	brotherhood
breakage	brigand	brother-
breaker	bright	in-law
breakfast	brighten-	brought
break-	ing	brow
fasted	brightens	brown
breaking	brighter	brouse
breakneck	brightest	bruise
bream	brightness	brunette
breast	brill	brunion
breastbone	brilliance	brunt
breast-pin	brilliant	brush
breast-plate	brim	brushwood
breastwork	brimless	brusque
breath	brine	brutal
breathe	bring	brutes

brutish	bungler	buying
bubble	bunion	by
buccaneer	bunk	bye
buck	bunker	bygone
bucket	buoy	by-lane
bucketfuls	buoyancy	by-name
buckle	buoyant	by-road
buckler	buphaga	bystander
buckram	bur	
buck-skin	burden	Cab
bud	bureau	cabal
budge	burglar	cabbage
budged	burgo-	cabin
buff	master	cabinet
buffalo	burial	cable
buffer	buried	cablet
buffet	burlesque	cabman
buffoon	burn	cachalot
bug	burnet	cachectic
buggy	burning	cachou
bugle	burnish	cackle
bugler	burnt	cad
buhl	burrow	cadaverous
build	burse	caddy
builder	burst	cadence
building	bury	cadets
bulb	busby	cadger
bulbous	bush	cadmium
bulge	bushman	cafés
bulk	busily	cage
bull	business	caique
bull-	business-	cairn
baiting	like	cajole
bulldog	buskin	cake
bullet	bust	calamine
bulletin	bustle	calamity
bully	busy	calando
bulrush	but	calcareous
bumkin	butcher	calculate
bump	butchery	calculated
bumper	butler	calculating
bumpkin	butt	calcula-
bun	butter	tions
bunches	butterfly	caldron
bunchy	button	calender
bundle	buttonhole	calenture
bundled	buttress	calf
bung	buxom	calibre
bungalow	buy	calico
bungle	buyer	caliduct

calin	canella	card
calipee	canine	cardinal
caliph	cannibal	care
calix	cannon	career
call	canny	careful
called	canoes	carefully
callers	canon	careless
calling	canonical	carelessly
callous	canopy	careless-
callousness	cant	ness
callow	canter	caress
callus	canticle	cargo
calm	canton	carman
calmer	cantor	carnage
calotype	canvas	carnal
calumniate	canvasser	carnival
calumnia-	cap	carvinora
tory	capable	carp
calumny	capacious	carpal
calvanism	capacity	carpenter
calvary	caparison	carpet
calve	cape	carpolite
calyx	caper	carriage
cam	capital	carrier
camber	capitalist	carrion
cambric or	capite	carrot
came	capoc	carry
camel	capon	carrying
cameo	caprice	carse
camera	capricious	cart
camp	caprine	cartage
campaign	capriole	cartel
campana	capsize	carter
camphor	capsized	cartilage
camphorate	captain	cartoon
can	caption	cartridge
canal	captious	cartwright
canard	captivate	carve
canary	captivat-	carvel
cancel	ing	carver
cancelled	captive	cascade
cancer	captivity	case
candid	captor	caseman
candidate	capture	caserate
candle	car	casement
candle-	caravan	caseous
stick	carbon	cash
candour	carbonic	cash-book
candy	carbonizing	cashed
cane	carcass	cashier

*See Preface

cashmere	cater	census
casino	catgut	cent
cask	cathedral	centage
casket	catholic	centen-
casque	catkin	arian
cassation	cattle	centenary
cassia	caucus	central
cassock	caudal	centre
cast	caught	centurion
castanets	cauf	centuries
castaway	caul	century
caste	causal	cerago
castellated	cause	ceramic
caster	caused	cerate
castigate	causeless	cere
castigation	caustic	cereal
casting	cauterize	cerebral
castle	caution	cerebrate
castor	cautionary	cerebration
castor-oil	cautious	ceremonial
casual	cavalcade	ceremonious
casuality	cavalier	ceremony
cat	cavalry	certain
catachres-	cave	certainly
tic	cavern	certainty
catacomb	cavernous	certificate
catacous-	cavil	certified
tics	cavity	certify
catagraph	cease	certitude
catalec-	cedar	cervine
tic	cede	cessation
catalogue	ceiling	cession
catalysis	celebrate	cessionary
cataphract	celebrated	cest
cataplasm	celebrating	cetate
catapult	celebration	cetic
cataract	celebrity	chad
catarrh	celerity	chafe
catastrophe	celery	chaff
catch	celestial	chaffinch
catchable	celibacy	chagrin
catching	celibate	chain
catchment	cell	chair
catechise	cellar	chairman
catechism	celt	chaise
catechist	cement	chaldron
cate-	cemetery	chalet
chumen	censer	chalk
category	censor	chalky
catenary	censorship	challenge

challenged	charmer	chest
chamade	charming	chestnut
chamber	charnel	cheval
chamber-	chart	chevalier
lain	charter	chew
chamomile	chartered	chewed
champ	char-woman	chica
champagne	chase	chicane
champion	chasing	chicken
champion-	chasm	chicory
ship	chaste	chide
chance	chat	chief
chancel	chateau	chiefly
chancery	chattel	chieftain
chandelier	chatter	child
chandler	chatter-	childhood
change	box	childish
change-	chatty	childless
able	chauffeur	children
changeful	cheap	chiliasm
changeless	cheaper	chill
changer	cheapest	chilly
channel	cheat	chiloma
chant	cheated	chime
chantry	check	chimera
chaos	check-book	chimney
chap	checkmate	chimpanzee
chapeau	cheek	chin
chapel	cheek-bone	china
chaperon	cheer	china-rose
chaperon-	cheerful	chine
age	cheerfully	chink
chaplain	cheerfulness	chintz
chaplet	cheery	chip
chapter	cheese	chipaxe
char	cheese-	chippy
character	monger	chiropodist
character-	chela	chirp
istic	chemical	chisel
character-	chemist	chiseled
ize	chemistry	chit
charade	chenille	chiton
chard	cheque	chivalric
charge	cherish	chivalrous
chargeable	cheroot	chivalry
charger	cherry	chlamys
chariot	cherub	chloral
charitable	cherubic	chlorate
chatity	chervil	chloride
charm	chess	chloroform

chlorotic	churchyard	cistern
chock	churl	citadel
chocolate	churlish	cite
choice	churn	citizen
choir	chute	citrate
choke	cicatrice	citric
choky	cicatrose	city
choler	cicerone	civic
cholera	cider	civil
cholic	cigar	civilian
chondrine	cilery	civility
choose	cimbal	civilization
choosers	cimolite	civilized
chop	cincture	clack
chopper	cinder	clad
choppy	cineration	claim
chopsticks	cipher	claimed
choral	circle	claimant
chord	circlet	clairvoy-
choriambus	circuit	ant
chorister	circular	clam
chorus	circulate	clamber
chowry	circula-	clammy
christ	tion	clamorous
christendom	circulator	clamour
christen-	circumam-	clamp
ing	bient	clams
christian	circumcise	clan
christianity	circumcision	clandes-
christian-	circumduct	tine
ize	circumference	clansman
christmas	circumflex	clap
christmas-	circumfluence	claque
tide	circumfluous	claquer
chromatic	circumnavi-	claret
chroma-	gate	clarify
trope	circumnavi-	clarion
chrome	gation	clash
chronic	circumrotary	clashing
chronicle	circumro-	clasp
chronogram	tation	class
chronology	circumscribe	classed
chrono-	circumscrip-	classic
meter	tion	classical
chum	circumstance	classify
church	circumstances	classman
churches	circumvent	clatter
churchman	circus	clause
church-	cirripede	claviary
member	cist	clavier

clavis	clique	cobbler
claw	cloak	cobra
clawing	clock	cobstone
clay	clog	cobweb
clayey	cloister	coca
clayish	close	cocaine
claymore	closed	cook
clay-pit	closer	cookade
clean	closely	cockatoo
cleaner	clot	cock-fight
cleanli-	cloth	cockle
ness	clothe	cockney
cleanly	cloud	cockroach
cleanse	clouds	cocoa
cleanser	cloudless	cocoon
clear	cloudy	coctile
clearance	clove	coction
clearer	cloven	cod
clear-	clover	code
headed	clown	codex
clearness	cloy	codicil
cleavable	club	codilla
cleave	clue	codle
cleaver	clump	coerce
cleft	clumsy	coercion
clergy	clung	coffee
clergyman	clusters	coffers
clerical	clutch	coffin
clerk	clutter	cog
clever	clyster	cogent
cleverest	coach	cogitation
clever-	coachman	cognate
ness	coact	cognizance
clew	coaction	cohabit
click	coadjutor	cohere
client	coagulate	coherently
cliff	coal	cohesion
climate	coal-gas	cohibit
climatic	coal-mine	cohort
climax	coalition	coif
climb	coarse	coil
climber	coast	coin
clime	coat	coinage
clinch	coated	coincidence
cling	coatee	coinhabi-
clinic	coax	tant
clinical	coaxing	coke
clino-	cob	colander
meter	cobalt	cold
clip	cobble	colder

* See Preface

colic	colt	commiserate
collaborate	columba	commissary
collabo-rator	columbic	commission
collapse	column	commission-aire
collar	coma	commit
collate	comb	committal
collation	*combat	committee
collect	combatant	commix
collected	combative	commodate
collection	combination	commodious
collective	combine	common
collec-tively	combined	commonly
collector	combustion	commoner
college	come	commonplace
collegian	comedian	common-sense
collet	comedy	commomwealth
collide	comet	commorant
collided	comfit	commotion
collie	comfort	commune
collier	comfortable	communicate
colliery	comfort-less	communication
colligate	comic	communion
colliga-tion	comical	community
collimation	coming	commutable
collimator	comma	compact
colliquant	command	compaction
collision	commandant	companion
colloquial	commanded	companionable
colloquy	commander	company
collude	commandment	comparable
colobus	commemorate	comparative
colon	commemora-tion	comparatively
colonel	commence	compare
colonial	commenced	comparison
colonist	commence-ment	compart
coloniza-tion	commencing	compartment
colony	commend	compass
colophon	commendable	compass-box
colorate	commendation	compassion
colossal	comment	compassion-ate
colour	commentary	compaternity
colourable	commentator	compatible
colour-blind	comments	compel
coloured	commerce	compellation
colourist	commercial	compend
	commination	compendium
	commingle	compensable

compensate
compensation
compete
competence
competent
competition
competitive
competitor
compile
compiling
complacence
complacent
complain
complainant
complaint
complement
complete
completely
completion
completive
complex
complexion
complexity
compliance
complicate
complicated
complica-
    tion
complicity
compliment
complimen-
    tary
compline
complot
comply
component
comport
comportment
compose
composed
composite
composition
compositor
compost
composure
compound
compound-
    able
compounder
comprehend

comprehen-
    sible
comprehen-
    sion
comprehen-
    sive
compress
compressed
compression
comprobate
compromise
compromit
compulsion
compunction
compute
comrade
comradeship
conation
concatenate
concave
concavity
conceal
concealed
concede
conceit
conceited
conceivable
conceive
concelebrate
concent
concentrate
concentra-
    tion
conceptacle
conception
conceptional
conceptive
concern
concerned
concerning
concert
concerted
concertina
concerto
concession
concierge
conciliar
conciliate
conciliation
concise

concisely
concision
conclave
conclude
conclusion
conclusive
conclusively
concoct
concocted
concoction
concoctive
concord
concordance
concordant
concorporate
concorpora-
    tion
concourse
concreate
concremation
concrescence
concrete
concretion
concubine
concur
concurred
concurrent
concurs
concuss
concussion
cond
condemn
condemn-
    able
condemna-
    tion
condensable
condensation
condense
condensed
condensity
condescend
condescension
condign
condiment
condite
conditement
condition
conditional
conditionary

conditory	confirmed	congress
condolatory	confiscate	congruence
condole	confiscation	congruity
condolence	confitent	conical
condone	confix	conjecture
conduce	conflagra-	conjugation
conducive	tion	conjure
conduct	conflict	connect
conduction	conflictive	connected
conductor	confluence	connecting
conduit	confluent	connection
condupli-	conflux	connive
cate	confluxable	connoisseur
cone	conform	connubial
confabulate	conformable	conoid
confamiliar	conformation	conquer
confect	conformer	conquered
confection	conformist	conquest
confec-	confound	conscience
tioner	confra-	conscientious
confederacy	ternity	conscien-
confederate	confront	tiously
confer	confronted	consciousness
conference	confuse	conscript
conferen-	confused	conscription
tial	confusing	consecrate
conferring	confusion	consecration
confess	confute	consecutive
confession	congeal	consent
confessor	congealment	consequence
confest	congenerous	consequent
confide	congenial	consequently
confided	congest	conservation
confidence	congestion	conservative
confident	congestive	conserve
confiden-	conglaciate	consider
tial	conglobe	considerable
confiding	conglom-	considerate
configura-	erate	consideration
tion	conglom-	considering
confinable	eration	consign
confine	conglutinate	consigned
confined	congratulate	consigna-
confinement	congratulated	ture
confinity	congratula-	consignment
confirm	tion	consist
confirmable	congregate	consistence
confirma-	congregated	consistency
tion	congrega-	consistent
confirmative	tion	consistently

consistory	contabulate	continuous
consolation	contact	continuously
consolatory	contagion	contort
console	contagious	contortion
consolidant	contain	contour
consolidate	containable	contra
consolida-	contaminate	contraband
tion	contami-	contract
consonant	nated	contracted
consort	contami-	contractible
conspectus	nation	contraction
conspicuous	contango	contractor
conspiracy	contemn	contradict
conspirator	contemper	contradiction
conspire	contemplate	contradictive
conspired	contemplat-	contradictory
constable	ed	contradis-
constancy	contempla-	tinction
constant	tion	contradis-
constantly	contemplative	tinguish
constellate	contempory	contrafissure
consternation	contempt	contralto
constituency	contemptible	contra-
constituent	contend	position
constitute	contendent	contrariant
constitution	content	contraries
constitu-	contented	contrariety
tional	contentment	contrariness
constrain	contention	contrary
constrained	contentious	contrast
constraint	conterminal	contrasting
constrict	contest	contrasts
constric-	contestation	contravene
tor	contested	contravention
construct	context	contretemps
constructed	contexture	contributary
construction	contignation	contribute
constructive	continence	contribution
construe	continent	contributor
consubstan-	continental	contrite
tial	contingence	contrition
consult	contingency	contrivance
consultation	contingent	contrive
consumable	continual	control
consume	continuance	controller
consumed	continuation	controversial
consummate	continue	controversy
consummation	continued	controvert
consumption	continues	contumacious
consumptive	continuity	contumacy

contumely	coolie	corneous
contuse	coop	corner
contusion	co-operate	cornered
conumdrum	co-opera-	cornet
convales-	tion	cornice
cence	co-operator	corniform
convales-	co-ordinate	cornine
cent	co-ordina-	cornist
convection	tion	cornucopia
convene	copal	corody
convenience	copatain	corolla
convenient	co-patriot	corollary
convent	cope	corona
conven-	copec	coronal
ticle	copestone	coronation
convention	coping	coroner
conventional	copious	coronet
converge	copper	corporal
convergence	copperas	corporate
cohversable	coppice	corporation
conversant	copse	corporeal
conversation	copula	corps
converse	copy	corpse
conversion	copyist	corpulence
convert	copyright	corpulent
converted	coquet	corpuscle
convex	coquetry	correct
convey	coracle	correction
conveyance	coral	correlate
convict	corant	correspond
convicted	corb	correspondent
convince	corban	corridor
convincible	cord	corroborant
convincing	cordage	corroborate
convive	corded	corrodent
convival	cordial	corrosive
convocate	cordiform	corrugate
convocation	cordon	corrupt
convoke	core	corruptible
convolve	co-respon-	corruption
convoy	dent	corsage
convulse	cork	corselet
convulsion	corked	corset
coo	corkscrew	cortège
cooing	corky	cortex
cook	cormorant	corticate
cookery	corn	cortile
cool	cornage	coruscate
cooler	corn-	corybantic
coolest	chandler	coseismal

oosey	course	cranny
cosinage	court	crape
cosmetic	courteous	crash
cosmopolitan	courtesy	crasis
cossack	courtier	cratch
cost	courtly	crate
costal	court-	crater
coster	martial	cravat
costly	court-	crave
costume	plaster	craven
cot	courtship	craving
coterie	cousin	crawl
cotidal	covenant	crax
cottage	cover	crayon
cottager	covering	craze
cotton	covert	crazed
cotyledon	coverture	crazy
couch	covet	creak
couchant	coveted	cream
cough	covetous	creamy
could	covetous-	crease
council	ness	create
councillor	covey	creating
count	cow	creation
countable	coward	creative
counte-	cowardice	creator
nance	cowardly	creature
counter	cowed	crèche
counteract	cowl	credence
counter-	cowry	credentials
balance	coxcomb	credit
counterfeit	coy	creditable
counterfoil	cozen	creditor
countermand	crab	credulous
countermine	crabbed	creed
counterpane	crack	creek
counterpart	cracker	creep
counterpoint	crackle	cremaillere
countersign	cradle	cremation
countess	craft	crenate
countless	crafty	crenature
countrified	crag	crenaux
country	cram	crepitate
coupee	cramp	crepon
couple	cramped	crept
couplet	crampoons	crescent
coupling	cranage	cress
coupon	cranberry	crest
courage	cranium	crestfallen
courageous	crank	cretated

crevice
crew
crib
cribbage
cribation
cricket
crime
criminal
criminally
crimp
crimson
crinoline
crinose
cripple
crisis
crisp
criterion
critic
critical
critically
criticise
criticised
criticism
critique
croak
croaky
crochet
crock
crockery
crocket
crocodile
crocous
croft
crook
crook-back
crooked
croon
crop
croquet
crosier
cross
cross-examination
cross-examine
crossing
cross-question
cross-road

crosswise
crotchet
crouch
croup
croupier
crow
crowbar
crowd
crowded
crown
crownless
crown-post
crown-prince
crown-wheel
croy
croze
crucial
crucible
crucifix
cruci-fixion
cruciform
crucify
crude
cruel
cruelty
cruet
cruise
crusier
crumb
crumble
crumbling
crupper
crusade
cruse
crush
crust
crustated
crusty
crut
crutch
crux
cry
crying
crypt
cryptic
crystal

crystallize
crystalization
cub
cubation
cubature
cubic
cubit
cuckoo
cucullate
cucumber
cud
cuddle
cuddy
cudgel
cue
cuff
cuirass
cuisine
culinary
cull
culminate
culmina-tion
culpable
culprit
cult
cultivate
cultivation
cultivator
cultural
culture
culvert
cumber
cumbrous
cumulate
cumulation
cumulus
cunning
cup
cupboard
cupel
cupid
cupola
cur
curable
curate
curative
curator
curb

See Preface

curcumine	cutting	dance
curd	cuttle	danced
curdle	cuvette	dancer
cure	cyanosis	dancing
curio	cycle	dander
curiosity	cycloid	dandle
curious	cyclone	dandy
curl	cyclopaedia	danger
curly	cyclops	dangerous
currant	cyclosis	dangle
currency	cylinder	dank
current	cyma	danseuse
curricle	cynache	dapedius
curriculum	cynic	dapple
currier	cynical	dare
curry	cynosure	daring
curse	cypress	dark
cursed	cyst	darken
cursitor		darkened
cursive	Dab	darkness
cursory	dabble	darksome
curt	dabster	darky
curtain	dace	darling
curtana	dactyl	darn
curtate	dad	dart
curtsy	dado	dash
curtilage	daft	dastard
curvated	dagger	dastardy
curvation	daggle	dastardly
curve	daguerreo-	data
curvet	type	dataria
cushion	daily	date
cusp	dainty	date-palm
cuspidal	dairy	dative
custard	dais	datum
custody	daisy	daub
custom	dale	dauby
customary	dalliance	daughter
customer	dally	daughters
custom-	dam	daunt
house	damage	dauntless
customs	damaging	davina
cut	damask	davits
cute	dame	daw
cuticle	damosel	dawdle
cutis	damp	dawk
cutlass	damper	dawn
cutler	damps	dawning
cutlery	damsel	day
cutlet	damson	daybreak

daylight	début	decoction
daytime	decade	decolorate
daze	decadence	decomplex
dazed	decalogue	decompose
dazzle	decamp	decomposition
deacon	decamped	decompound
deaconess	decampment	decorate
dead	decant	decorated
deaden	decay	decoration
dead-letter	decayed	decorative
dead level	decease	decorous
deadly	deceased	decorum
deadness	deceit	decoy
deaf	deceitful	decrease
deafen	deceitfully	decree
deafening	deceive	decrepit
deal	deceived	decrepitate
dealers	december	decrown
dealing	decency	decrusta-
dealt	decennary	tion
dean	decent	decry
deanery	deception	decursive
deanship	deceptive	dedicate
dear	decide	dedicated
dearth	decided	dedication
death	deciduous	dedicatory
deathless	decile	dedimus
deathlike	decimal	deduce
deathly	decimate	deduct
debacchate	decimation	deduction
debacle	decimator	deed
debar	decipher	deedless
debark	decipherable	deem
debarka-	deciphering	deep
tion	decision	deepen
debase	decisive	deepest
debasement	deck	deface
debate	declaim	defalcate
debating	declamation	defamation
debauch	declamatory	defame
debauchery	declaration	default
debenture	declare	defeat
debilitate	declared	defeated
debility	declension	defeating
debit	declinable	defect
debitor	declination	defective
debonair	decline	defence
débris	declined	defenced
debt	declivity	defendant
debtor	decoct	defender

defensive	delibate	demoniac
defer	deliberate	demonic
deference	deliber-	demonism
deferent	ately	demonstrate
deferred	deliberation	demonstrated
defiance	delicacy	demonstra-
defiant	delicate	tion
deficiency	delicately	demonstra-
deficient	delicious	tive
deficit	deligation	demonstra-
defied	delight	tor
defile	delighted	demoraliza-
define	delightful	tion
definite	delineate	demoralize
definitely	delineation	demotic
definition	delinquent	demulcent
deflect	delirious	demur
deflux	delirium-	demurrage
deforce	deliver	den
deform	deliverance	denarius
deformation	delivery	denial
deformity	dell	denim
defraud	delta	denizen
defray	delude	dennet
deft	deluge	denomin-
defunct	delusion	able
defy	delve	denominate
degenerate	demagogue	denomination
degeneration	demand	denomina-
degradation	demandant	tive
degrade	demarka-	denotable
degrading	tion	denotation
degree	demean	denote
dehisce	demeanour	denounce
dehort	demented	denounced
deicide	demerit	denouncing
deifica-	demersed	dense
tion	demi	density
deify	demi-god	dent
deign	demise	dental
deism	demiss	dentate
deist	demit	dentation
deity	demobilise	dented
deject	democracy	dentifrice
dejection	democrat	dentil
delapse	democratic	dentine
delate	demolish	dentist
delay	demolished	dentistry
delectable	demolition	denude
delegate	demon	denunciate

denuncia-tion	deprive	designer
deny	depths	desipient
denying	deputation	desirability
deodorize	depute	desirable
deoppilate	deputy	desire
depaint	deracinate	desired
depart	derail	desirous
departed	derange	desist
department	derelict	desisted
departure	deride	desk
depend	derision	desolate
dependable	derivate	desolation
depended	derivation	despair
dependence	derivative	despairing
dependent	derive	despatch
depict	derm	desperado
depicted	dermal	desperate
depicting	dermatology	desperately
depicture	derogate	desperation
depilate	derogation	despicable
depilatory	derogatory	despisable
deplete	derrick	despise
depleted	derringer	despite
depletion	descant	despoil
depletive	descend	despond
deplorable	descendant	despondence
deplore	descendent	despondency
depone	descension	despondent
depopulate	descent	despot
deport	describable	despotism
deportment	describe	dessert
deposal	description	destemper
depose	descriptive	destinate
deposit	descry	destination
depositors	desecrate	destiny
depôt	desecration	destitute
deprave	desert	destitution
depraved	deserted	destroy
depravity	deserter	destroyable
deprecate	desertion	destroyed
deprecated	deserve	destroying
deprecation	deserved	destructible
depreciate	deservedly	destruction
depredate	desiccate	destructive
depress	design	desultory
depressed	designate	detach
depression	designation	detached
depriva-tion	designa-tor	detachment
	designed	detail
		detailed

detain
detained
detainment
detect
detection
detective
detent
detention
deter
deteriorate
deteriora-
    tion
determent
determin-
    able
determinate
determina-
    tion
determine
determined
deterration
deterred
detersion
detest
detestable
detested
dethrone
dethrone-
    ment
detonate
detonation
detort
detortion
detour
detract
detraction
detractive
detrain
detriment
detrimental
detrude
deuce
deuterogamy
devastate
devastation
develop
development
devest
deviate
deviation

device
devil
devilment
devilry
devious
devisable
devise
deviser
devoid
devolution
devolve
devote
devoted
devotion
devotional
devour
devouring
devout
dew
dewdrop
dewlap
dewy
dexter
dexterity
dexterous
diabetes
diabolical
diaconal
diadem
diadrom
dieresis
diagnose
diagnosis
diagonal
diagram
diagraph
dial
dialect
dialogue
diameter
diamond
diaphragm
diary
diatribe
dibble
dice
dictaphone
dictate
dictated
dictating

dictation
dictatorial
diction
dictionary
dictum
did
didactic
didactyl
diddle
diduction
die
died
die-sinker
diet
dieted
dietetic
differ
difference
differences
different
differently
differential
differentiate
difficult
difficulty
diffidence
diffident
diffuse
diffused
diffusion
dig
digest
digestible
digestion
digestive
digger
dight
digitalis
digitate
diglyph
dignified
dignify
dignitary
dignity
digress
dike
dilapidate
dilapidated
dilapida-
    tion

dilate	dirty	discharged
dilated	disability	discinct
dilatory	disable	disciple
dilemma	disabuse	disciplin-
dilettante	disadvantage	arian
diligence	disadvantageous	discipline
diligent	disaffect	disciplined
dill	disaffected	disclaim
dilute	disaffection	disclama-
dilution	disaffirm	tion
dim	disagree	disclose
dime	disagreeable	discolora-
dimensions	disagreement	tion
diminish	disallow	discolour
diminished	disannul	discomfit
diminution	disappear	discomfort
diminutive	disappearance	discommend
dimity	disappoint	discommode
dimple	disappoint-	discommon
din	ment	discommunity
dine	disapproba-	discompose
dingle	tion	discomposure
dingy	disappropriate	disconcert
dinner	disapproval	disconcertion
dint	disapprove	disconnect
diocesan	disarm	disconnected
diocese	disarmament	disconnec-
diorism	disarray	tion
diota	disassociate	disconsolate
dioxide	disaster	discontent
dip	disastrous	discontented
diphtheria	disattach	discontinue
diphthong	disavow	discord
diploe	disband	discordance
diploma	disbar	discordant
diplomacy	disbelief	discount
diplomate	disbelieve	discourage
diplomatic	disbeliever	discouraged
dipody	disburden	discourage-
dipso-	disc	ment
mania	discandy	discourse
dipteral	discard	discoursing
dire	discarded	discourteous
direct	discarnate	discourtesy
direction	discern	discover
director	discernible	discovered
directory	discerning	discoveries
dirge	discernment	discredit
dirk	discession	discreditable
dirt	discharge	discreet

discrepant
discrete
discretion
discretion-
    ary
discrimi-
    nate
discrimi-
    nation
discursive
discuss
discussed
discussion
disdain
disdainful
disease
diseased
disembark
disembarrass
disembody
disemployed
disenchant
disendow
disengage
disengaged
disentangle
disentitle
disestablish
disestablish-
    ment
disesteem
disfavour
disfranchise
disfranchise-
    ment
disgarnish
disgorge
disgrace
disgraceful
disguise
disguised
disgust
disgusted
disgust-
    ingly
dish
dishabilitate
dishabille
dishearten
dishevel

dishonest
dishonesty
dishonour
dishonour-
    able
disillusion
disincli-
    nation
disincline
disinfect
disinherit
disinheri-
    tance
disinter
disinterested
disjoin
disjoined
disjoint
disjointed
disjunction
disk
dislike
disliked
dislocate
dislocation
dislodge
disloyal
disloyalty
dismal
disman
dismantle
dismask
dismast
dismay
dismember
dismiss
dismissed
dismissal
dismount
disobedience
disobedient
disobey
disoblige
disobliging
disorder
disorgani-
    zation
disorganize
disown
disparage

disparity
dispassion
dispel
dispelling
dispensable
dispensary
dispensation
dispense
dispensing
dispermous
dispersal
disperse
dispersed
dispersion
dispirit
dispirited
displace
displacement
displant
display
displayed
displease
displeasure
disport
disposal
dispose
disposed
disposition
dispossess
dispossession
disposure
dispraise
disprofit
disproof
disproportion
disproval
disprove
dispute
disqualify
disquiet
disquietous
disquietude
disquisition
disregard
disregarded
disreputable
disrepute
disrespect
disrespect-
    ful

disrobe	distinction	divination
dissatis-	distinctive	divine
faction	distinguish	diving
dissatisfied	distinguished	divinity
dissatisfy	distinguish-	division
dissect	ing	divisor
dissection	distitle	divorce
dissemble	distort	divorced
disseminate	distortion	divulge
dissension	distract	dizziness
dissent	distracted	dizzy
dissenter	distraction	do
dissert	distrain	doab
dissever	distraught	dobhash
dissidence	distress	docent
dissimilar	distressed	docile
dissimila-	distribute	docility
tion	distributed	dock
dissimulate	distributer	docket
dissimula-	distribution	doctor
tion	district	doctrine
dissipate	distrust	document
dissipation	distrustful	dodder
dissociate	disturb	dodge
dissoluble	disturbance	doe
dissolute	disturbed	does
dissolution	disunion	doeskin
dissolve	disunite	doff
dissolvent	disuse	dog
dissolving	disvalue	doge
dissonance	ditch	dogged
dissonant	ditch-water	doggerel
dissuade	ditto	dogma
dissuasion	ditty	dogmatic
dissyllabic	diurnal	dogmatist
distaff	divan	dohl
distance	dive	doily
distant	diver	doings
distaste	diverge	doit
distasteful	divergency	dolce
distemper	diverse	dole
distemper-	diversify	doleful
ance	diversion	doll
distend	diversity	dollar
distention	divert	dolly
distil	divest	dolorous
distillate	divide	dolphin
distillation	divided	dolt
distillery	dividend	domain
distinct	dividual	dome

domestic	dowers	drawling
domical	down	drawn
domicile	downcast	dray
dominance	downfall	drayman
dominant	down-gyved	drazel
dominate	down-	dread
domination	hearted	dreadnought
domineer	downpour	dreadful
dominical	downright	dream
dominion	downstairs	dreamer
domino	downtrod	dreamland
don	downwards	dreamy
donation	downy	drear
done	dowry	dreary
donkey	doxology	dredge
donna	doze	dredger
donor	dozen	dregs
donzel	drab	drench
doom	drabble	drenched
doomed	drachm	dress
doomsday	draco	dressed
door	draft	dresser
door-step	drag	dressing
doorway	draggle	dressmaker
doric	dragon	drew
dormant	dragoon	drib
dormitory	drail	dribble
dornic	drain	drift
dot	drainage	drifting
dotage	drake	drill
dotard	dram	drilling
dote	drama	drink
dotes	dramatic	drinkable
double	dramatist	drinking
doublet	dramatize	drip
doubling	drape	drip-stone
doubloon	draper	drive
doubt	drapery	drivel
doubted	drastic	driver
doubtful	draught	driving
doubtless	draughts	drizzle
douche	draughty	droil
dough	draw	droit
doughty	drawback	droll
dove	drawbridge	drollery
dovetail	drawer	dromedary
dovetailed	drawing	drone
dowager	drawing-	droop
dowel	room	drooping
dower	drawl	drop

* see Preface

dropping	dulcet	dynasty
drops	dulcimer	dysnomy
drop-scene	dull	dyspepsia
dropsical	dullard	dysthetic
dropsy	dullest	
dross	duly	Each
drought	dumb	eager
drove	dumb-bells	eagerly
drover	dumfound	eagle
drown	dummy	ear
drowned	dump	earache
drowsy	dumpling*	earing
drub	dun	earl
drudge	dunce	earldom
drudgery	dune	earlier
drug	dungeon	earliest
drugget	dunt	early
druggist	dupe	earn
druids	duplex	earnest
drum	duplicate	earnestly
drummer	duplica-	earning
drunk *	tion	ear-ring
drunkard	duplicity	earshot
druse	durable	earth
dry	durance	earthly
dryad	duration	earthquake
drying	during	earthwork
dual	dusk	earthy
dualist	dusky	earwig
dub	dust	ease
dubiate	dustbin	easel
dubious	duster	easier
ducal	dust-hole	easily
ducat	dusty	east
duchess	duteous	easter
duck	dutiable	easterly
duct	dutiful	eastern
ductile	duty	eastward
ductility	duumvir	easy
dudgeon	dwarf	eat
due	dwarfish	eatable
duel	dwell	eau
duellist	dweller	eaves
duello	dwelling	eavesdrop
duenna	dwindle	ebb
duet	dye	ebbing
duffer	dyer	ebon
dug	dynamic	ebony
duke	dynamite	eboule-
dukedom	dynamo	ment

* See Preface

ebriety	eerie	ejaculated
ebullient	effable	ejaculation
ecarté	efface	eject
ecbatic	effect	ejected
ecbole	effective	ejection
eccentric	effectual	eke
eccentricity	effeminacy	elaborate
ecclesia	effeminate	elaboration
ecclesiastic	effervesce	elaborator
ecclesiasti-	efferves-	elaine
cal	cence	eland
echinate	efficacious	elapidation
echo	efficacy	elapse
echometry	efficiency	elapsed
eclectic	efficient	elastic
eclipse	effigy	elasticity
eclogue	effloresce	elate
economical	efflores-	elated
economize	cence	elater
economiz-	effluvium	elation
ing	efflux	elbow
economy	effort	elder
ecstasy	effortless	elderly
eczema	effranchise	eldest
edacious	effrontery	elect
edacity	effulge	election
eddy	effulgence	elevtive
eden	effuse	elector
edental	effusion	electric
edge	egest	electrician
edged	egg	electricity
edgewise	egg-cup	electrophone
edging	egilops	elegance
edible	ego	elegant
edict	egoist	elegantly
edifice	egotist	elegiac
edify	egotistic	elegist
edit	egregious	elegy
edition	egress	element
editor	egression	elementary
editorial	egret	elements
educate	egrette	elephant
education	eider	elevate
educational	eidograph	elevated
educator	eight	elevation
educe	eighteen	elevator
educt	eighty	eleven
eduction	eikon	elf
eel	either	elfin
eel-skin	ejaculate	elfish

elicit	embarrass	emotion
elide	embarrassed	emotional
eligible	embarrass-	empale
elimate	ment	empannel
eliminate	embassy	empark
elimination	embattle	emperil
elision	embellish	emperor
elite	embellishment	emphasis
elixir	embers	emphatic
elk	embezzle	emphati-
ellipse	embezzlement	cally
ellipsis	embezzler	empire
elliptic	embezzling	emplastic
elm	emblazon	employ
elocution	emblem	employé
eloge	emblematic	employee
elogy	embodiment	employees
eloin	embody	employer
elongate	embogue	employment
elongation	embolden	emporetic
elope	embolism	emporium
eloped	emboss	empower
elopement	embossed	empress
eloquence	embow	emptied
eloquent	embower	emptiness
else	embrace	empty
elsewhere	embraces	empryean
elucidate	embrasure	emu
elucidation	embrocate	emulate
elude	embrocation	emulation
elusion	embroider	emulous
elutriate	embroil	emulsion
elvan	embryo	emuscation
elves	emerald	enable
elysian	emerge	enact
elysium	emergiencies	enactment
emaciate	emergency	enamel
emaciation	emersion	enamour
emaculate	emery	enanthema
emanate	emetic	enate
emanation	emigrant	encage
emancipate	emigrate	encamp
emancipa-	emigration	encampment
tion	eminence	encase
embalm	eminent	encashment
embalmed	emissary	encaustic
embank	emission	enchain
embar	emit	enchant
embargo	emolliate	enchantment
embark	emollient	encircle

encircled
enclasp
enclosure
encompass
encompass-
    ment
encore
encored
encounter
encountered
encourage
encouraged
encourage-
    ment
encroach
encroach-
    ment
encrust
encumber
encyclopedia
end _ or _
endear
endearment
endeavour
ended
enderon
endless
endogamy
endorse
endow
endower
endowment
endurable
endurance
endure
enema
enemy
energetic
energize
energy
enervate
enervation
enfeeble
enfetter
enforce
enfranchise
engage
engagement
engender
engine

engineer
engineering
engird
engirdle
engrave
engraver
engross
enhance
enhanced
enigma
enjoin
enjoy
enjoyable
enjoying
enkindle
enlarge
enlighten
enlightened
enlist
enliven
enmity
ennoble
enormity
enormous
enough
enrage
enrapt
enrich
enrichment
enripen
enrobe
enrockment
enrol
enrolment
ensample
ensconce
enshrine
enshroud
ensign
enslave
ensnarl
ensue
entail
entailment
entangle
entastic
enter
entered
enteric
entering

enterprise
entertain
entertaining
entertainment
entheal
enthral
enthrone
enthusiasm
enthusiast
entice
enticed
enticer
entire
entirely
entirety
entitle
entitled
entity
entoil
entomb
entrails
entrain
entrammel
entrance
entranc-
    ingly
entrap
entreat
entrochal
entry
entwine
entwist
enubilate
enumerate
enumeration
enunciate
enunciation
envelop
envelope
envenom
enviable
envious
environ
environment
envoy
envy
enwreath
eon
epact
epagoge

* See Preface

eparch	equipment	esquire
epaule	equipoise	essay
epaulette	equitable	essayed
epergne	equity	essence
ephelis	equivalent	essential
ephemera	equivoke	establish
ephod	era	establishment
epic	eradiate	estate
epicarp	eradicate	esteem
epicure	erase	estimable
epidemic	erased	estimate
epidermis	erect	estimation
epidote	erected	estrange
epigene	erection	estrange-
epigram	ereption	ment
epigraph	ergot	estray
epilepsy	erica	estuary
epileptic	ericaceous	etch
epilogue	ermine	etched
epiphany	erodent	eternal
epiphora	erosion	eternally
epiphysis	erotic	eternity
epiplexis	err	ether
episcopal	errand	ethereal
episcopy	errant	ethic
episode	erratic	ethical
epispastic	erroneous	ethnic
epistle	error	etiquette
epistrophe	erudite	etymology
epitaph	erudition	eucharist
epithet	erupt	euchology
epitome	eruption	euchre
epoch	erysipelas	euge
epode	escalade	eugenic
epos	escapade	eulogic
equable	escape	eulogize
equal	escaped	eulogy
equally	escapement	eunuch
equality	escarp	euphonic
equalize	escheat	euphuism
equanimity	eschew	eureka
equate	escort	eutonia
equation	escritoire	evacuate
equator	escutcheon	evacuation
equestrian	esoteric	evade
equilibrium	especial	evaded
equine	especially	evanesce
equinox	espionage	evangel
equip	espouse	evangelic
equipage	espy	evangelist

evangelize	example	exemplar
evanish	examination	exemplify
evaporate	exarticu-	exempt
evaporation	lation	exemption
evasion	exasperate	exercise
eve	exasperation	exercises
even	excavate	exert
evening	excavation	exertion
event	exceed	exhale
eventful	exceedingly	exhaust
eventide	excel	exhausted
eventual	excellence	exhaustion
eventually	excellency	exhaustively
ever	excellent	exhaustless
evergreen	except	exhibit
everlasting	exception	exhibiting
evermore	exceptional	exhibition
eversion	excess	exhilarate
evert	excessive	exhilarating
every	exchange	exhilaration
everybody	exchequer	exhort
every-day	excise	exhortation
everywhere	excision	exigent
eviction	excite	exile
evidence	excitement	exist
evident	exclaim	existence
evil	exclamation	exists
evince	exclude	exit
evocation	excluded	exodus
evoke	exclusion	exogen
evolution	exclusive	exonerate
evolve	excogitate	exorable
evolvent	excommunicate	exorbitant
evolving	excommuni-	exorcise
evulsion	cation	exotic
ewe	excoriate	expand
ewer	excruciate	expanded
exacerbate	exculpate	expanse
exact	exculpation	expansion
exactly	excursion	expansive
exacting	excursive	expect
exaction	excuse	expectant
exactor	execrate	expectation
exaggerate	execration	expected
exaggeration	execute	expectorate
exalt	execution	expedience
exalted	executioner	expedient
examination	executive	expedition
examine	executor	expel
examiner	exegesis	expend

expenditure	extortion	fact
expense	extortionary	faction
expenses	extra	factious
expensive	extract	factitious
experience	extracted	factor
experiment	extraction	factory
expert	extractor	factotum
expiate	extradition	faculty
expire	extraneous	fad
explain	extraordinary	fadge
explanation	extravagance	fading
explicate	extravagant	faecal
explicit	extreme	faeces
explode	extremely	fag
exploration	extremity	fagot
explore	extricate	fail
explosion	extrication	failing
exponent	extrinsic	failure
export	extrusion	fain
expose	exuberance	faint
exposed	exude	faintly
exposition	exult	fair
expostulate	exultant	fairly
exposure	exultation	fairway
expound	exuviation	fairy
express	eye	fairy-tale
expressed	eye-ball	faith
expression	eyelet	faithful
expressly	eye-lid	faithfully
expulsion	eyes	faithfulness
expurgate	eyesight	faithless
exquisite	eye-water	fake
extempore	eyrie	falcade
extend		falcate
extending	Faba	falchion
extension	fable	falcon
extensively	fabric	faldstool
extent	fabrication	fall
extenuate	fabricator	fallacy
extenuation	fabulous	fallen
exterior	façade	fallow
exterminate	face	false
extermina-	faced	falsehood
tion	facet	falsely
external	facetious	falsetto
extinct	facial	falsify
extinguish	facile	falsity
extirpate	facilitate	falter
extol	facility	fama
extort	fac-simile	fame

famed	fasten	feast
fameless	faster	feasting
familiar	fastest	feat
familiarly	fastidious	feather
familiarity	fastigiate	feathered
family	fasting	feature
famine	fastness	featured
famish	fat	february
famishing	fatal	federal
famous	fatally	federate
famously	fatalism	federation
fan	fatalist	fee
fanatic	fate	feeble
fancied	fated	feed
fancy	fateful	feeder
fancy-ball	father	feel
fane	fatherless	feet
fang	fatherly	feign
fan-light	fathom	feigned
fan-tail	fathomable	feint
fantasia	fatigue	felicitate
fantastic	fatling	felicity
fantasy	fatted	feline
far	fatten	fell
farce	fatty	feller
farcical	fatuity	fellow
fardel	faucal	fellow-
fare	faucet	citizens
farewell	fault	fellow-
farm	faultless	creature
farmer	faulty	fellowship
farming	faun	felon
farm-house	fauna	felonious
farm-yard	fauteuil	felony
faro	favose	felt
farrier	favour	felucca
farrow	favourable	female
farther	favourably	feminine
farthing	favoured	fen
fasces	favourite	fence
fascets	favus	fencible
fascial	fawn	fencing
fasciated	fay	fend
fascinate	feal	fender
fascination	fealty	ferment
fashion	fear	fermentation
fashion-	fearful	fern
able	fearless	fernery
fashioned	fearlessly	ferocious
fast	feasible	ferocity

ferret	fiendish	fining
farreted	fierce	finish
ferrule	fiercely	finishing
ferry	fiery	finite
fertile	fife	fiord
fertility	fifteen	fir
fertilize	fifth	fire
ferule	fig	fire-arm
fervency	fight	fireman
fervent	fighter	fire-screen
fervently	figment	fire-wood
fervid	figural	firing
fervour	figurative	firkin
festal	figure	firm
fester	figured	firmament
festival	figure-head	firmness
festive	filament	first
festivity	filbert	firstborn
festoon	filch	first-fruits
fetal	filched	firstly
fetch	file	fisc
fête	filial	fiscal
fetich	filagree	fish
fetter	filings	fisher
fettered	fill	fishery
fettle	filler	fish-hook
feu	fillet	fish-
feud	filly	kettle
feudal	film	fishy
fever	filmy	fisk
feverish	filter	fissure
few	filth	fist
fiasco	filthy	fistula
fib	filtrate	fit
fibre	fin	fitch
fibrous	final	fitched
fichu	finally	fitful
fickle	finance	five
fiction	financed	fix
fictitious	financial	fixature
fiddle	financier	fixed
fiddler	finch	fixedly
fidelity	find	fixture
fidget	finding	flabber-
fidgety	fine	gasted
field	finery	flabby
field day	finesse	flaccid
fielder	finger	flackie
field-works	finger-bowl	flag
fiend	finical	flageolet

flagitious
flagon
flagrant
flag-ship
flag-staff
flail
flake
flaky
flam
flambeau
flamboyant
flame
flaming
flammable
flamy
flanch
flange
flank
flankards
flannel
flap
flapped
flapping
flare
flash
flashed
flashes
flashy
flask
flasket
flat
flatten
flatter
flattered
flattering
flattery
flatulent
flaunt
flaunted
flavour
flaw
flax
flea
fleak
fleam
fleck
fledge
flee
fleece
fleecy

fleet
fleeter
flesh
fletch
fletcher
flew
flex
flexibility
flexible
flexile
flick
flies
flight
flighty
flimsy
flinch
fling
flint
flinty
flip
flippant
flirt
flirtation
flit
flitch
flitter
float
flotage
flock
flock-bed
floe
flog
flood
flooded
flood-gate
floor
flooring
flop
flora
floral
florescence
floret
florid
florin
florist
floss
flota
flotant
flotilla
flounce

flounder
flour
flourish
flout
flow
flower
flowery
flowing
fluctuate
fluctua-
    tions
flue
fluent
fluff
fluid
fluke
flume
flummery
flunkey
flurry
flush
fluster
flute
fluted
flutter
flutter-
    ingly
fluvial
flux
fluxation
fluxion
fly
flying
foal
foam
fob
focal
focus
fodder
foe
foeman
fog
foggy
fog-signal
foible
foil
foin
foist
fold
folded

folding	forced	forester
foliage	forcibility	forestry
foliate	forcible	foret
folio	forcing	foretaste
folk	forcing-	forethought
follia	house	forfeit
follow	forcipation	forfeited
follower	ford	forfeiture
following	fore	forge
folly	forebode	forgery
foment	foreboding	forget
fomentation	forecast	forgetful
fond	forecastle	forgetful-
fondest	foreclose	ness
fondness	foreclosed	forging
fondle	foreclosure	forgive
fondus	foredoom	forgiveness
font	forefather	forgiveing
fontal	forefend	fork
food	forefinger	forked
foodless	forego	forlay
fool	foreground	forlorn
foolery	forehead	form
foolish	foreign	formal
foolishly	foreigner	formality
foot	forejudge	formalize
foot-ball	foreknow	formation
foot-bath	forel	formative
foot-bridge	foreland	formed
footing	forelock	former
foot-lights	foreman	formerly
footman	foremast	formication
foot-pad	foremost	formidable
footprint	forenoon	forming
footstep	fore-ordain	formless
foot-stool	forespeak	formula
foot-warmer	foreprize	formulate
fop	forerun	fornicate
foppish	forerunner	fornication
for	foresaid	fornix
forage	foresee	fors
foramen	foreseeing	forsake
foraminous	foreseen	forsaken
foray	foreshadow	forsooth
forbade	foreship	forswear
forbear	foreshorten	fort
forbearance	foreshow	forte
forbid	foresight	forth
forbidden	forest	forthcoming
force	forestall	forthwith

fortieth	foy	fremescent
fortifica-	foyer	french
tion	fracas	frequency
fortify	fraches	frequent
fortitude	fracid	fresco
fortnight	fraction	fresh
fortress	fractious	freshen
fortuitous	fracture	freshman
fortuity	fragile	fret
fortunate	fragment	fretful
fortune	fragrancy	fretwork
forty	fragrant	friar
forum	frail	fribble
forward	fraise	friction
forwardness	fraised	friday
forwards	frame	friend
fosse	framer	friendless
fossil	framework	friendliness
fossilization	framing	friendly
fossilize	franc	friendship
fossorial	franchise	frieze
foster	frank	frigate
foster-child	frankly	fright
foul	frankin-	frightened
foulard	cense	frightful
found	frantic	frigid
foundation	franticly	frigidity
founder	frantically	frill
foundering	frap	fringe
foundry	fraternal	frippery
foundling	fraternally	frisk
fount	fraterniza-	frisky
fountain	tion	frith
fountain-	fraud	fritter
pen	fraudlence	frivolous
four	fradulent	frizzle
fourbe	fraught	fro
fourfold	fray	frock
fourneau	freak	frog
fourpenny	freckle	frolic
four-poster	free	from
fourscore	free-city	frond
four-square	freedom	frondous
fourteen	free-hand	frons
fourth	freely	front
fowl	freeman	frontal
fowler	freemason	frontier
fox	free-will	frontispiece
foxed	freeze	frost
fox-hound	freight	frosted

frosty	funk	gala
froth	funnel	galea
frow	funniest	galimatias
froward	funny	gall
frown	fur	gallant
frowned	furacious	gallantry
frowning	furbelow	galleon
frozen	furcate	gallery
fructed	furious	galley
fructify	furl	gallic
fructuous	furlong	galling
frugal	furnace	gallon
frugality	furnish	galloon
fruit	furniture	gallop
fruit-bud	furrier	galloping
fruitful	furrow	gallows
fruitfulness	further	galoche
fruity	furthermore	galore
frustrate	furtive	galvanism
frustrated	fury	galvanized
frustration	furze	gambit
fry	fuse	gamble
frying-pan	fused	gambler
fucate	fusee	gambling
fudge	fusil	gamboge
fuel	fusillade	gambol
fugacious	fusion	game
fugacity	fuss	gamester
fugitive	fust	gammon
fugue	fustic	gamut
fuguist	fustigate	gander
fulfil	futile	gang
fulgent	futility	ganger
full	future	gangrene
fuller	futurist	gangrenous
fulminate	futurity	gangway
fulsome		gantlet
fume	Gab	gaol
fumid	gabble	gap
fumigate	gable	gape
fun	gad	garb
funambu-	gaff	garbage
list	gaffle	garble
function	gag	garden
fund	gage	gardener
fundamental	gaiety	gare
funeral	gaily	garfish
fungi	gain	gargle
fungoid	gait	garish
fungus	gaiter	garland

garlic	geat	gerant
garment	geese	germ
garner	gehenna	german
garnet	gelastic	germinate
garnish	gelatine	germination
garniture	geld	gerund
garret	gelder-rose	gestic
garrison	gelid	gesticulate
garrot	gem	gesticula-
garter	geminate	tion
garth	gemmation	gesture
gas	gender	get
gas-engine	genealogy	geysers
gaseous	genera	ghastly
gash	general	ghaut
gasify	generality	ghost
gas-jet	generalize	ghostly
gasket	generally	ghoul
gas-meter	generate	giant
gasogene	generation	giantess
gasometer	generous	gibbet
gasoscope	genesis	gibbose
gasp	genet	gibe
gastric	genial	giblets
gastritis	genitive	gibs
gas-works	geniture	giddy
gate	genius	gift
gate-house	genoese	gifted
gateman	genre	gigantic
gate-way	genteel	giggle
gather	gentile	gild
gathered	gentility	gilder
gathering	gentle	gilding
gaucherie	gentleness	gill
gaud	gentlefolks	gilt
gaudy	gentleman	gimbals
gauffer	gentlemen	gimlet
gauge	gentlewoman	gimmal
gaunt	gentry	gimp
gauze	genuflec-	gin
gauzy	tion	ginger
gavel	genuine	gingham
gavotte	geocyclic	gingle
gawk	geode	gipsy
gawn	geography	giraffe
gay	geology	gird
gaze	geometer	girder
gazelle	geometry	girdle
gazette	geonomy	girl
gear	georgic	girlhood

girlish	glimpse	gnomon
girt	glint	gnostic
girth	glissade	gnu
gist	glist	go
give	glitter	goad
gives	gloaming	goaf
glacial	gloat	goal
glaciate	globate	goat
glacier	globe	goatherd
glad	globous	goat-skin
gladden	globulous	gobble
glade	globule	gobbled
gladiator	glome	gobelin
gladsome	glomerate	goblet
glair	gloom	goblin
glaive	gloomy	god
glamour	glorifica-	godchild
glance	tion	goddess
glanced	glorify	godfather
gland	glorious	godhead
glanders	glory	godless
glandule	gloss	godlike
glare	glossy	godly
glared	glottis	godmother
glaring	glove	godroon
glaringly	glow	godson
glass	glowing	gog
glass-	gloze	goglet
cutting	glucose	going
glasses	glue	goitre
glass-house	glued	gold
glassware	glum	gold-beater
glass-work	glume	gold-dust
glassy	glumous	golden
glaucous	glut	goldfinch
glaze	glutinate	gold-fish
glazier	glutinous	gold-foil
glazing	glutton	gold-plate
gleam	gluttony	goldsmith
glean	glycerine	golf
gleaner	glyph	gome
glebe	glyphic	gondola
glebous	glyphograph	gondolier
glee	glyptics	gone
glene	gnarl	gong
glenoid	gnash	good
glib	gnat	good-bye
glide	gnaw	good-humour
glim	gneiss	goodly
glimmer	gnome	good-nature

good-sense	graduate	grater
good-speed	graduated	gratification
goodwill	graduation	gratified
goose	graff	gratify
gooseberry	graft	grating
gore	grail	gratis
gorge	grain	gratitude
gorgeous	grained	gratuitous
gorgeously	graining	gratuity
gorgon	grains	gratulate
gorilla	gramaphone	gratulation
goring	grammar	grave
gormand	gramma-	gravel
gormandize	tical	gravel-pit
gorman-	granary	gravita
dized	grand	gravitate
gorse	grandchild	gravitation
gory	grand-	gravity
gosling	daughter	gray
gospel	grand-duke	grayish
gossamer	grandee	graze
gossip	grandeur	grazer
goth	grandly	grease
gothic	grand-	greasy
gouda	mother	great
gouge	grandson	greater
gourd	grand-stand	greatest
gourmand	grange	greatly
gout	granger	great-seal
gouty	granite	greaves
govern	granivorous	grebe
governess	grant	grecian
government	granted	greed
governor	granular	greedy
gown	granulate	greek
grab	granule	green
grace	grape	green-back
graceful	grape-shot	greenfinch
graceful-	grape-vine	greengage
ness	graphic	green-house
graceless	graphite	green-room
grace-note	graphium	green-tea
graces	grapnel	green-wood
gracile	grapple	greet
gracious	grasp	greeting
graciously	grasping	gregarious
gradation	grass	gremial
grade	grasshopper	grenade
gradual	grate	grenadier
gradually	grateful	grey

grice	grounds	guipure
griddle	group	guise
gride	grouping	guitar
gridiron	grouse	gular
grief	grout	gulf
grievance	grove	gulf-stream
grieve	grovel	gull
grieved	grow	gullet
grievous	growl	gullibility
griffin	growled	gully
grill	grown	gulosity
grillage	growth	gulp
grille	grub	gum
grilse	grubble	gum-arabic
grim	grudge	gumbo
grimace	gruel	gum-boil
grime	gruesome	gumlac
grimy	gruff	gummous
grin	grum	gun
grind	grumble	gun-barrel
grinder	grumbler	gun-boat
grindstone	grumous	gun-cotton
grip	grunt	gunner
gripe	grunter	gunnery
grisette	gryposis	gunpowder
grist	guano	gunshot
gristle	guarantee	gunsmith
grit	guard	gunwale
gritty	guarded	gurgle
grizzle	guardsman	gurnet
groan	guberna-	gush
groat	torial	gushing
grocer	gudgeon	gusset
grocery	guerdon	gust
grog	guess	gut
groin	guest	gutta percha
groom	guhr	gutter
groomed *	guidance	gutteral
groove	guide	guy
grope	guided	gybe
gross	guild	gynasium
grossest	guile	gymnast
grot	guileless	gymnic
grotto	guilloche	gynecian
grotesque	guillotine	gypsum
ground	guilt	gyrate
groundage	guiltless	gyre
ground-	guilty	gyroscope
floor	guinea	gyrose
groundless	guinea-pig	gyve

* See Preface

Haberdasher	halliard	haquebut
habiliment	hall-mark	harangue
habit	hallow	harass
habitable	hallowed	harbinger
habitant	hallucina-	harbour
habitation	tion	hard
habitual	halo	harden
habituate	halt	hardened
habitue	halter	hard-hearted
hachure	halting	hardly
hack	halve	hardness
hackle	ham	hardship
haddock	hamate	hardware
hade	hame	hardy
hades	hamite	hare
haema-	hamlet	harem
chrome	hammer	hark
haemal	hammock	harl
haft	hamous	harlequin
hag	hamper	harlot
haggard	hamster	harm
haggle	hamstring	harmattan
haggler	hand	harmful
hagiarchy	hand-bill	harmless
hagiology	hand-book	harmonic
hail	handcuff	harmonious
hair	handed	harmonist
hair-breadth	handfast	harmonium
hairless	handful	harmonize
hair-pin	handicap	harmony
hairy	handiwork	harness
hake	handker-	harp
halberd	chief	harpoon
halcyon	handle	harried
hale	hand-screw	harrow
half	handsel	harry
half-bred	handsome	harsh
half-caste	handwriting	hart
half-hearted	handy	harvest
half-length	hang	harvester
half-moon	hanging	hash
half-note	hangman	hasp
half-pay	hangnail	hassock
halfpenny	hanker	haste
half-sister	hankle	hastily
half-witted	hap-hazard	hasty
halibut	hapless	hat
halicore	happen	hat-band
halituous	happened	hatch
hall	happy	hatchet

* The hook is permitted here.

hatchment	healthier	height
hatchway	healthy	heighten
hate	heap	heinous
hath	hear	heir
hatred	heard	heir-
hatter	hearing	apparent
hauberk	hearken	heiress
haughty	hearsay	heir-loom
haul	hearse	heir-
haunch	heart	presumptive
haunt	heartache	held
haunted	hearth	helocoid
haunting	heartily	heliograph
hautboy	heartless	heliotrope
hauteur	heartlessness	helix
haut-gout	heart-sick	hell
have	hearty	hellish
haven	heat	helm
haversack	heater	helmet
havoc	heath	helmsman
haw	heathen	help
hawk	heather	helpful
hawker	heating	helpless
hawse	heave	helplessness
hawthorn	heaven	helpmate
hay	heavenly	helve
haycock	heavenward	hem
hay-fever	heavily	hematine
hay-field	heaving	hemi
hazard	heavy	hemicrania
hazardous	hebe	hemina
haze	hebetate	hemiopia
hazel	hebrew	hemiplegia
hazy	hecatomb	hemisphere
he	heck	hemlock
head	heckle	hemmorrhage
headache	hectic	hemp
header	hector	hem-stitch
headland	heddles	hen
head-line	hederal	hence
headlong	hedge	henchman
head-piece	hedgehog	hen-coop
head-	hedgerow	hendiadys
quarters	hedonic	henna
headsman	heed	hepatic
head-stone	heedless	heptade
heal	heel	heptagon
healer	heel-piece	heptarchy
health	hegemony	heptateuch
healthful	heifer	her

herald	hexagon	hink
heraldry	hexameter	hinny
herb	hiatus	hint
herbaceous	hibernate	hip
herbage	hiccough	hippocratic
herbal	hid	hippodrome
herbalist	hidden	hircin
herbescent	hide	hircus
herculean	hideous	hire
herd	hidrotic	hired
herdman	hierarch	hireless
here	hieratic	hireling
hereafter	hieroglyph	hirsute
hereditary	hierogly-	his
heredity	phic	hiss
heresy	hierology	hist
heretic	hieroscopy	historian
hereto	high	historical
herewith	high-day	history
heritage	higher	hit
hermaphro-	highest	hitch
dite	highland	hithermost
hermetic	highly	hitherto
hermit	high-mass	hitherward
hermitage	high-minded	hive
hernia	highness	hoar
hero	high-priest	hoard
heroic	high-road	hoarded
heroine	high-tide	hoarder
heroism	high-time	hoarfrost
heron	high-water	hoarse
hero-worship	highway	hoary
herpetology	hilarious	hoax
herring	hilarity	hob
herse	hill	hobble
herself	hillock	hobbler
hesitant	hilltop	hobby
hesitate	hilly	hobgoblin
hesitatingly	hilt	hobit
hesitation	hilted	hobnail
hesper	hilum	hobnob
hesperian	him	hock
hest	himself	hockey
hetarism	hind	hockle
heterodox	hinder	hocus
heteronomy	hinderance	hod
heteroscian	hindermost	hodge
hew	hindu	hoe
hexachord	hindustanee	hog
hexade	hinge	hogget

hogshead	honorarium	horseback
holden	honorary	horse-
hoist	honour	breaker
hold	honourable	horse-flesh
holder	honoured	horsefly
holdfast	hood	horse-guards
holding	hooded	horse-hair
hole	hoodwink	horseman
holiday	hoof	horsemanship
hollow	hook	horse-pond
holly	hook-pin	horse-race
holm	hooky	horsewhip
holocaust	hoop	hortative
holograph	hoopoe	horticulture
holometer	hoot	hose
holster	hop	hosiery
holy	hop-back	hospice
homage	hope	hospitable
home	hoped	hospital
home-born	hopeful	hospitality
homeless	hopeless	host
homelot	hoping	hostage
homely	hoplite	hostel
home-office	hoppet	hostler
homeopathic	hopple	hot
homeopathy	hopscotch	hot-bed
home-rule	hop-vine	hotel
home-sick	hop-yard	hot-house
home-spun	horal	hot-press
homestead	horary	hotspur
homeward	horde	houdah
homicidal	horizon	hough
homicide	horizontal	hound
homiletics	horn	hour
homily	horned	hour-glass
hominy	hornet	houri
hommock	hornfoot	hourly
homogeneal	hornito	house
homograph	hornpipe	house-agent
homonym	horography	house-boat
homoousian	horoscope	household
hone	horrent	householder
honest	horrible	housekeeper
honestly	horrid	houseless
honey	horrified	house-maid
honey-bag	horrify	house-
honey-bee	horrisonous	warming
honey-comb	horror	housewife
honey-dew	horse	housing
honeymoon	horses	hove

how	hungry	hymn
however	hungrily	hymnology
howitzer	hunt	hyperborean
howl	huntress	hyper-
howling	hurdle	critical
hoy	hurds	hyphen
hub	hurl	hypnotic
huckaback	hurled	hypnotise
huckle	hurricane	hypochondria
huckster	hurried	hypocrisy
huddle	hurriedly	hypocrite
huddled	hurry	hypocriti-
hue	hurt	cal
huff	hurtful	hypodermic
hug	hurtle	hypothec
huge	husband	hypothesis
hugely	husbanding	hysteria
hugeness	husbandman	hysterical
hulk	husbandry	
hull	hush	I
hum	husk	iambic
human	husky	iambus
human-being	hussar	ibex
humane	hustle	ibis
humanely	hut	ice
humanitar-	hutch	iceberg
ianism	hux	ice-boat
humanity	hyacinth	ice-bound
human-	hyades	ice-cream
nature	hybrid	ice-field
humble	hydra	ice-floe
humbug	hydrate	ice-house
humectant	hydraulic	ichor
humective	hydrogen	ichthyocol
humeral	hydrology	ichthyosis
numerus	hydrometer	icicle
humid	hydropathic	icing
humidity	hydropathy	icon
humiliate	hydrophane	icono-
humiliation	hydrophobia	clasm
humility	hydroscope	ictus
hummock	hydrostatic	icy
humorist	hyemal	idea
humorous	hyemation	ideal
humour	hyena	idealist
hump	hyetal	ideality
humpback	hyetograph	idealize
hunch	hygiene	ideation
hundred	hylicist	identical
hunger	hymen	identify

identity	illimited	immaterial
ideograph	illision	immaterial-
ideology	illiterate	ist
idiocrasy	ill-nature	immature
idiocy	illness	immaturity
idiom	illogical	immeasur-
idiomatic	illude	able
idiopathy	illume	immediate
idiosyn-	illuminate	immediately
crasy	illumina-	immemorial
idiot	tion	immense
idiotcy	illumi-	immensely
idiotic	nator	immensity
idiotically	illusion	immerge
idle	illusionary	immerse
idler	illusive	immersion
idol	illustrate	immesh
idolater	illustration	immethod-
idolatry	illustrator	ical
idolize	illustrious	immigrant
idolized	image	immigrate
idyl	imagery	immigration
if	imaginable	imminence
igneous	imaginary	imminent
ignescent	imagination	imminution
ignipotent	imaginative	immiscible
ignite	imagine	immission
ignoble	imago	immit
ignomin-	imband	immobility
ious	imbecile	immoderate
ignominy	imbellic	immoderately
ignoramus	imbibe	immoderation
ignorance	imbibed	immodest
ignorant	imbitter	immolate
ignore	imbosom	immolation
ilex	imbricate	immomen-
iliad	imbrication	tous
ilium	imbroglio	immoral
ill	imbrue	immorality
illapse	imbue	immortal
illaqueate	imbued	immortality
illation	imburse	immortalize
illative	imitate	immortelle
illegal	imitated	immovable
illegibility	imitating	immunity
illegible	imitation	immure
illegitimate	imitative	immutability
illiberal	immaculate	immutable
illicit	immanation	imp
illimitation	immanent	impacable

impact	imperforate	impolite
impair	imperial	impolitic
impale	imperialism	imponder-able
impalm	imperil	
impalpable	imperious	imporous
impalsy	imperishable	import
impanate	impermanent	importance
impanel	impermeable	important
imparadise	impersonal	importantly
imparity	impersonate	importation
imparl	impersona-tion	importing
impart		importunate
imparted	imperspicuity	importune
impartial	imperspic-uous	impose
impassable		imposition
impassion	imperti-nence	impossibility
impassioned		impossible
impassive	impertinent	impost
impaste	impertran-sible	imposthumate
impasto		impostor
impatience	imperturba-bility	imposture
impatient		impotent
impatronize	imperviable	impound
impeach	impervious	impoverish
impeachment	impetuous	impracti-cable
impearl	impetus	
impecca-bility	impiety	imprecate
	impinge	imprecation
impeccant	impious	impregnable
impecunious	impish	impregnate
impede	implacable	impress
impediment	implant	impresses
impels	implantation	impressible
impellent	implausible	impression
impen	impleach	impressive
impend	implead	impressive-ness
impending	implement	
impendent	impletion	imprest
impenetra-bility	implex	imprint
	implexion	imprinted
impenetrable	implicate	imprison
impenitence	implication	imprison-ment
impenitent	implicit	
impennate	implicitly	improbability
imperative	implied	improbable
imperatively	implore	impromptu
impercep-tible	implored	improper
	imploringly	impropriate
imperfect	imply	impropriety
imperfection	implying	improve

improved	inaquate	incidence
improvement	inarable	incident
improver	inarticu-	incidental
improvi-	late	incinerate
dence	inarticu-	incipiency
improvident	lation	incipient
improvise	inasmuch	incircle
imprudence	inattention	incise
imprudent	inattentive	incised
impudence	inaudible	incision
impudent	inaugural	incite
impugn	inaugurate	incivility
impulse	inauguration	incivism
impulsion	inbred	inclement
impulsive	incalcu-	inclination
impunity	lable	incline
impure	incandescent	inclined
impurity	incantation	inclip
imputable	incapable	inclose
impute	incapacious	inclosed
in	incapaci-	inclosing
inability	tate	inclosure
inaccessi-	incapacity	incloud
ble	incarcerate	include
inaccuracies	incarn	inclusive
inaccurate	incarnate	incogitance
inaction	incarna-	incogitant
inactive	tion	incognito
inactivity	incase	incoherent
inadequate	incasement	incoinci-
inadequately	incaution	dence
inadhesion	incautious	incoinci-
inadvertent	incavated	dent
inaffable	incavation	incombus-
inamorato	incendiar-	tible
inane	ism	income
inaniloquent	incendiary	incommen-
inanimate	incense	surable
inanimation	incensive	incommen-
inanition	incentive	surate
inapplicable	inception	incommoda-
inappreciable	inceration	tion
inapprehen-	incessant	incommode
sible	incessantly	incommodious
inapproach-	incest	incommuni-
able	inch	cative
inappro-	inchest	incommutable
priate	inchoat	incomparable
inapt	inchoation	incompati-
inaptitude	inchpin	bility

incompatible
incompetence
incompetent
incomplete
incomplex
incompliable
incompliance
incompliant
incomposite
incomprehen-
 sible
incomprehen-
 sion
incomprehen-
 sive
incomputable
inconceivable
inconclusive
incondensible
incondite
inconfor-
 mable
inconformity
inconfusion
incongenial
incongeni-
 ality
incongruity
incongruous
inconnexion
inconse-
 quence
inconsequent
inconsider-
 able
inconsiderate
inconsider-
 ately
inconsis-
 tence
inconsistent
inconsolable
inconspic-
 uous
inconstancy
inconstant
inconsum-
 able
inconsummate
incontested

incontin-
 ently
incontroll-
 able
inconve-
 nience
inconvenient
inconver-
 sable
incorporate
incorpora-
 tion
incorporeal
incorrect
incorrectly
incorrigible
incorrupt
incorruption
incrassate
increase
incredulity
incredulous
increment
increscent
incriminate
incrust
incubate
incubation
incubator
incubus
inculcate
inculpate
incult
incumbent
incur
incurable
incursion
incurvate
incuss
indebted
indebtedness
indecent
indeciduous
indecipher-
 able
indecision
indecisive
indeclin-
 able
indecorous

indecorum
indeed
indefati-
 gable
indefen-
 sible
indefinite
indelible
indelicate
indemnity
indent
indented
indenture
independence
independent
indescri-
 bable
indestruc-
 tible
indetermi-
 nate
index
indicant
indicate
indication
indicative
indicator
indicatory
indiction
indictment
indifference
indifferent
indigence
indigene
indig-
 enous
indigent
indigested
indigestible
indigestion
indignant
indignantly
indignation
indignity
indigo
indirect
indirection
indiscernible
indiscipline
indiscreet

indiscrete
indiscretion
indiscrim-
    inate
indispen-
    sable
indispose
indisposed
indisposi-
    tion
indispu-
    table
indissoluble
indistinct
indistinction
indite
inditement
individual
individuality
indocile
indolence
indolent
indorse
indorsed
indorsement
indraught
indrawn
indubious
induce
induced
inducement
induct
induction
inductor
indue
indulge
indulgence
indulgent
indurate
induration
industrial
industrious
industry
indwelling
inebriate
ineffability
ineffable
ineffaceable
ineffective
ineffectual

inefficacious
inefficient
inelegance
inelegant
ineligible
ineloquent
inept
inequality
inequitable
inert
inertia
inestimable
inevident
inevitable
inevitably
inexact
inexcusable
inexhal-
    able
inexhausted
inexhaus-
    tible
inexorable
inexpensive
inexperience
inexperienced
inexpert
inexpiable
inexplica-
    bility
inexplicable
inexplicit
inexpressi-
    ble
inexpressive
inextri-
    cable
infallible
infamous
infamy
infancy
infant
infantile
infantry
infatuate
infatuation
infect
infection
infectious
infective

infelicity
infer
inference
inferential
inferior
inferiority
infernal
inferno
infest
infeudation
infidel
infidelity
infiltrate
infinite
infinites-
    imal
infinitive
infini-
    tively
infirm
infirmary
infirmity
infix
inflame
inflamm-
    able
inflamma-
    tion
inflate
inflation
inflect
inflection
inflexible
inflict
infliction
inflores-
    cence
influence
influential
influenza
influx
infold
inform
informal
inform-
    ality
information
informed
informer
infraction

inframundane	inharmonious	inoculate
infrangible	inhere	inoculation
infrequency	inherence	inoffensive
infrequent	inherent	inofficial
infringe	inherit	inordinate
infringement	inheritance	inordinately
infumate	inheritor	inorganic
infuriate	inhibition	inquest
infuriated	inhospitable	inquire
infuriating	inhuman	inquirer
infuscate	inhume	inquiries
infuse	inimical	inquiry
infused	inimitable	inquisition
infuser	iniquitous	inquisitive
infusing	iniquity	inroad
infusion	initial	insane
ingate	initiate	insanity
ingeminate	initiated	insanitary
ingenerate	initiative	insatiable
ingenious	inject	inscribe
ingenuity	injection	inscription
ingenuous	injudicious	inscrutable
ingestion	injunction	insecable
inglorious	injure	insect
ingot	injurious	insecure
ingraft	injury	insecurity
ingrafted	injustice	insensate
ingrafting	ink	insensible
ingrain	inkling	insentient
ingrained	inky	inseparable
ingrappled	inland	insert
ingrate	inlaid	insertion
ingratiate	inlay	inset
ingratitude	inlet	inshrine
ingredient	inmate	inside
ingress	inmost	insidious
ingrowing	inn	insight
inguinal	innate	insignia
ingulf	inner	insignificant
inhabit	innermost	insincere
inhabitable	innervation	insincerity
inhabitant	innocence	insinuate
inhabited	innocent	insipid
inhalant	innocuous	insipient
inhalation	innovate	insist
inhale	innovation	insisted
inhaler	innuendo	insistent
inhaling	innumerable	insnare
inharmonic		insobriety

insolate	insuffi-	intercept
insolation	ciency	intercepted
insolence	insufficient	interception
insolent	insular	intercession
insoluble	insulate	interchange
insolvent	insulation	interchange-
insomnia	insult	able
inspan	insulted	intercipient
inspect	insuperable	interclude
inspection	insupportable	intercommuni-
inspector	insurable	cation
inspiration	insurance	intercom-
inspire	insure	munion
inspiring	insurmount-	intercostal
inspirit	able	intercourse
inspissate	insurrection	intercutan-
instability	insuscep-	eous
instal	tible	interdict
installation	intact	interest
instalment	intaglio	interested
instance	intake	interesting
instances	intangible	interfere
instant	integral	interference
instantly	integrate	interfluent
instantan-	integrity	interim
eous	integument	interior
instead	intellect	interjacent
instep	intellectual	interject
instigate	intellec-	interjection
instigation	tuality	interjunc-
instil	intelligence	tion
instillation	intelligible	interlace
instinct	intelligibly	interlay
instinctive	intemperance	interleaf
instinc-	intemperate	interleave
tively	intend	interline
institute	intended	interlineal
instituting	intenerate	interlink
institution	intense	interlock
institu-	intensify	interlo-
tional	intensity	cution
instruct	intent	interlope
instruction	intention	interloper
instrument	intention-	interlude
instrumental	ally	inter-
insuavity	inter	marriage
insubord-	interact	intermarry
ination	interaction	intermeddle
insufferable	interagent	intermedial
insufferably	intercede	intermediate

interment
intermica-
  tion
intermi-
  gration
intermin-
  able
interminate
intermina-
  tion
inter-
  mingle
intermission
intermit
intermittent
intermix
intermon-
  tane
intermun-
  dane
intermuta-
  tion
intern
internal
interna-
  tional
internecine
internode
internuncio
interoscu-
  lant
interpellate
interpene-
  trate
interplay
interplead
interpolate
interpose
interposit
interpret
interpreta-
  tion
interrogate
interroga-
  tion
interroga-
  tive
interrupt
interruption
interscind

interscribe
intersect
intersecting
intersection
intersperse
interspersed
interstice
intertrop-
  ical
intertwine
interval
intervene
interview
interviewed
interviewer
intervolve
interweave
interwoven
intestate
intestine
intimacy
intimate
intimately
intimation
intimidate
intimida-
  tion
into
intolerable
intoler-
  ance
intolerant
intonate
intonation
intone
intorsion
intort
intoxicate
intoxica-
  tion
intractable
intramural
intransient
intransitive
intransmut-
  able
intrench
intrench-
  ment
intrepid

intrepidity
intricate
intrigue
intrinsic
introduce
introducing
introduc-
  tion
introspect
introversion
introvert
intrude
intrusion
intrust
intuition
intuitive
inumbrate
inundate
inurbane
inure
inustion
inutility
inutterable
invade
invalid
invalidate
invaluable
invariable
invasion
invasive
invective
inveigh
inveigle
invent
invented
invention
inventive
inventor
inventory
invermina-
  tion
inverse
inversion
invert
invest
investigate
investi-
  gated
investi-
  gation

investiture	irreconcil-able	islam
investment	irrecover-able	island
inveterate	irrecusable	isle
invidious	irredeem-able	isolate
invigorate		isolation
invincible	irrefragable	isonomy
inviolable	irregular	isosceles
inviolate	irregularity	issue
invisibility	irrelative	issued
invisible	irrelevant	isthmus
invitation	irreligion	it
invite	irreligious	italian
invocate	irremiss-ible	itch
invocation		item
invoice	irremovable	iterant
invoke	irremuner-able	iteration
involun-tary		itinerant
involute	irreparable	itinerary
involution	irreprehen-sible	itinerate
involve		itself
involved	irrepressible	ivory
invulnerable	irreproachable	ivy
inward	irreptitious	Jabber
inwardly	irresistable	jacent
inwrought	irresolute	jackal
iodine	irresolution	jacket
ion	irrespective	jacquard
iota	irresponsi-bility	jaculate
irascible		jaculation
irate	irrespon-sible	jade
ire		jag
ireful	irretriev-able	jagged
iridescence		jail
iriscope	irreverence	jailer
irish	irreverent	jakes
irksome	irrevocably	jam
iron	irrigate	jemb
iron-bound	irrigation	jangle
iron-founder	irrision	january
iron-work	irritable	janus
ironic	irritant	japanese
irony	irritate	jar
irradiance	irritated	jargon
irradiate	irritation	jasmine
irradicate	irruption	jasper
irrational	is	jaundice
irreclaim-able	ischial	jaunt
	isinglass	jaunty
		javelin

jaw	jolting	jurisprudent
jawbone	jostle	jurist
jay	jot	juror
jealous	journal	jury
jealously	journalism	just
jealousy	journalist	justice
jeer	journey	justifi-
jeered	joust	cation
jejune	jovial	justify
jellied	jowl	justly
jelly	joy	jut
jeremy	joyance	jute
jeopardize	joyful	juvenile
jeopardised	joyfully	juvenility
jeopardy	joyless	juxtaposition
jerk	joylessly	
jerkin	joyous	Kaiser
jersey	jubilant	kale
jest	jubilation	kaleido-
jester	jubilee	scope
jesting	judaism	kali
jet	judge	kam
jetty	judgment	kama
jew	judicatory	kangaroo
jewel	judicature	kayak
jeweller	judicial	kayle
jewess	judicious	keck
jib	judiciously	keckle
jig	jug	kedge
jilt	juggle	keel
jingle	juggler	keen
jingled	jugular	keep
jingoism	juice	keeper
job	juicy	keeping
jobber	jujube	keepsake
jockey	july	keg
jocose	jumble	keir
jocosely	jump	kelk
jog	jumper	kell
joggle	junction	kelp
join	juncture	kelt
joinery	june	kemp
joint	jungle	kennel
jointed	junior	kept
jointure	junket	kerasine or
joist	jurat	kerf
joke	juridical	kern
jollity	jurisdiction	kernel
jolly	jurispru-	kerosene
jolt	dence	ketch

ketchup	klepto-mania	kraal
kettle	knab	krang
kevel	knack	kremlin
key	knag	kurd
key-board	knap	kurkee
keynote	knapple	kyriologic
kibble	knapsack	
kibe	knarl	Labarum
kick	knave	labefac-tion
kicked	knavish	label
kid	knead	labial
kidnap	knee	laboratory
kidney	kneed	laborious
kill	kneel	labour
killed	kneeling	labourer
killow	knell	labouring
kiln	knew	labrose
kilo-gramme	knicker-bockers	labyrinth
kilt	knife	lac
kin	knight	lace
kind	knighted	lacerate
kinder	knighthood	laceration
kinder-garten	knightly	lachesis
kindle	knit	lachrymal
kindling	knitted	lachrymose
kindly	knitting	lacing
kindness	knittle	laciniate
kindred	knob	lack
kine	knock	lackadai-sical
kinema	knocker	lackey
king	knoll	laconic
kingdom	knop	laconism
kingly	knot	lacquer
kink	knotty	la-crosse
kino	knout	lactrine
kinsman	know	lactate
kiosk	knowing	lacteal
kipe	knowledge	lactescent
kipper	known	lactic
kirk	knubs	lactine
kiss	knuckle	lactoscope
kissed	kobil	lacuna
kit	kobold	lacunose
kitchen	koff	lad
kite	kohl	ladder
kith	koth	lade
kitten	koul	ladle
kive	koumiss	lady

lady-day	landing	lass
lady-like	landlord	lassitude
lady-love	landmark	lasso
ladyship	landscape	last
lag	landslide	lasted
laggard	land-tax	lasting
lagoon	lane	latch
laic	langate	latchet
laid	language	late
lair	languid	latent
laird	languish	lateral
laity	langour	lath
lake	laniate	lathe
lallation	lank	lather
lamb	lantern	latin
lambent	lanyard	latest
lambskin	lap	latitude
lame	lapdog	latten
lameness	lapel	latter
lamella	lapful	lattice
lament	lapidary	laud
lamentable	lapis	laudable
lamenta-	lappet	laugh
tion	lappior	laughable
lametta	lapse	laughingly
lamia	lapsed	laughter
lamina	lapstone	launch
laminable	larboard	laundress
laminate	larceny	laundry
lamish	lard	laurel
lammas	large	lava
lamp	largely	lavatory
lampas	large-	lave
lampate	hearted	lavender
lampblack	large-	laver
lampic	minded	lavish
lamplight	larger	lavishly
lampoon	largess	law
lanary	largest	law courts
lanate	largition	lawful
lance	largo	lawless
lancer	lark	lawn
lancet	larrup	lawn-tennis
lancinate	larry	lawsuit
land	larum	lawyer
land-agent	larvated	lax
landau	laryngitis	laxation
landed	larynx	laxity
lander	lascivious	lay
landholder	lash	layer

laying	legato	lettering
layman	legend	lettuce
lazy	legendary	leucous
lea	legging	levant
leach _or_	legibility	levee
lead	legible	level
leader	legion	lever
leaf	legislate	levigate
leafy	legislation	levity
league	legislature	levogyrate
leak	legist	levy
leaky	legitimate	lewd
leal	legitimation	lexicon
leam	legitimist	liability
lean _or_	leisure	liable
leaning	lemma	lier
leap	lemon	libation
leaped	lemonade	libel
learn	lend	libellous
learned	lender	liberal
learner	lending	liberality
learning	length	liberate
learnt	lengthen	liberation
lease	lengthy	liberator
leash	lenient	liberty
least	lenitive	libra
leat	lenity	library
leather	lens	libration
leave	lent	license
leaven	lenten	licensed
leaving	lentil	licentiate
lecher	lentor	licentious
lectern	leo	lich
lection	leopard	lichen _or_
lecture	leper	lichenous
ledge	lepid	lichgate
ledger	leprosy	licit
lee	leprous	lick
leech _or_	less	lictor
leek	lessen	lid
leer	lessened	lie
leet	lesson _or_	lief
left	lest	liege
leg	let	lien _or_
legacy	letch	lieutenant
legal	lethal	life
legality	lethargy	lifeless
legate	letter	lifelong
legatee	letter-box	lift
legation	lettered	ligament

ligature	lioness	lively
light	lionize	liver
lighted	lip	livery
lighten	lipogram	livid
lighter	lippitude	living
lightly	liquate	livraison
lightning	liquation	lizard
ligneous	liquer	llama
legnine	liquid	load
lignite	liquidate	loaf
like	liquida-	loafer
likeable	tion	loam
likelihood	liquor	loath
likely	liquorice	loathe
liken	lirocone	loathing
likeness	lisp	loaves
lilt	list	lob
lily	listen	lobby
limaceous	listened	lobe
limation	listing	lobster
limb	listlessness	local
limber	litany	locality
lime	literal	locate
lime-light	literally	locating
limit	literary	location
limitation	literate	loch
limited	literature	lock
limn	lith	locked
limp	lithe	locker
limpet	lithic	locket
limpid	lithoglyph	lock-jaw
linament	lithograph	lock-out
linch	lithology	locksmith
linden	lithotint	locomo-
line	litigable	tion
lineament	litigant	locomotive
linen	litigate	locus
liner	litigation	locust
linger	litigious	lode
lingering	litmus	lodge
lingual	litotes	lodger
linguist	litter	lodgment
link	littered	loft
linn	little	log
linnet	littoral	log-book
linoleum	liturgy	loggan
linseed	live	loggia
lint	lived	logic
lintel	livelihood	logical
lion	livelong	logman

logos	lounge	lunacy
lohock	lounged	lunar
loimik	louse	lunary
loin	lout	lunate
loiter	lovable	lunatic
loll	love	lunch
lone	lovely	luncheon
lonely	lover	lung
lonesome	loving	lunge
long	low	lunt
longer	lower	lupine
longevity	lowered	lupus
longevous	lowering	luroh
longing	lowest	lure
longitude	lowland	lurid
long-	lowlander	lurk
sighted	lowly	luscious
loof	loyal	lust
look	loyalist	lustre
looked	loyalty	lustrous
looking	lozenge	lusty
lookout	lubric	lute
loom	lubricate	luther
looming	lubrica-	lutheran
loon	tion	luxuriant
loop	lubricator	luxurious
loophole	lucernal	luxury
loose	lucid	lyam
loosen	lucifer	lyceum
loot	luck	lychnobite
lop	luckless	lye
loquacious	lucky	lying
loquacity	lucre	lymph
lord	ludicrous	lynch
lordly	lues	lynched
lordship	luff	lynx
lore	lug	lyre
lorgnette	luggage	lyric
lorn	lugger	lysis
lorry	lugubrious	lyssa
lose	lukewarm	lyterian
loss	lull	
losses	lumbago	Mab
lost	lumbal	macadamize
lot	lumber	macaroni
lotion	lumbri-	mace
lottery	cal	macerate
lotus	luminary	maceration
loud	luminous	machine
louder	lump	machinery

mackerel	maintained	mandamus
mackintosh	mainten-	mandarin
mackle	ance	mandate
macled	maize	mandible
macrocosm	majestic	mandoline
mactation	majesty	mandrel
mad	majolica	manducate
madam	major	mane
madcap	majority	manequin
madder	make	manful
madeira	make-believe	manfully
mad-house	makeshift	magnate
madid	making	mange
madman·	malady	manger
madness	malaria	mangle
madonna	malarial	man-hole
madrigal	malcontent	manhood
maelstrom	male	mania
magazine	malediction	maniac
magenta	malefactor	manicure
maggot	malevolent	manicured
magic	malic	manicurist
magical	malice	manifest
magician	malicious or	manifesta-
magilp	malign	tion
magisterial	malignant	manifold
magistrate	malig-	maniglions
magnanim-	nantly	manilla
ity	malinger	maniple
magnanimous	mall	manipulate
magnate	malleable	manipula-
magnet	malleation	tion
magnetic	mallet	mankind
magnetism	mallow	manliness
magnetize	malt	manly
magnificent	maltose	manna
magnifi-	maltreat	manner
cently	mamelon	mannerism
magnify	mammal	manoeuver
magnitude	mammi-	manoeuver-
mahogany	ferous	ing
maid	mammon	manor
maiden	mammoth	manor-house
maidenhood	man	manse
mail	manacle*	mansion
maim	manage	manslaughter
maimed	management	man's self
main	manager	mantel
main-land	manageress	mantel-
maintain	manche	piece

* The omission of "a" in this and other outlines
is optional.

mantiger	martin	matinée
mantle	martinet	matrass
manual	martyr	matriar-
manufactory	martyrdom	chal
manufacture	marvel	matriculate
manufac-	marvellous	matricu-
turer	mascle	lation
manure	masculine	matrimony
manuscript	mash	matrix
many	mask	matron
map	masked	matronal
maple	mason	matronly
mar	masonic	matted
maraud	masque	matter
marauding	masquerade	mattock
marble	mass	mattress
marc	massacre	mature
march	massacred	maturity
marcid	massage	maud
mare	massive	maul
margin	mast	maulstick
marginal	master	maunder
margode	mastered	mausoleum
marine	masterly	mauve
mariner	master-	mavis
marionettes	piece	maw
mark	mastery	maxillar
marker	mastic	maximize
market	masticate	maximum
marking	mastication	may
marl	mastiff	may-day
marline	masty	may-morn
marmalade	mat	mayor
marmot	matadore	mayoress
maroon	match	may-queen
marplot	matchless	maze
marque	matchlock	mazy
marquee	mate	me
marquis	mater	mead
marred	material	meadow
marriage	materially	meagre
married	material-	meal
marrow	ism	mealy
marry	materialist	mean
marsh	materialized	meaning
marshal	maternal	meanly
marshy	maternity	meant
mart	mathematics	meantime
martello	matin	meanwhile
martial	matinal	measles

measurable	meliorate	mercenary
measure	melioration	mercer
measurement	mellow	mercery
measures	melodeon	merchant
meat	melodious	merciful
meatus	melodrama	merciless
mechanic	melodra-	mercilessly
mechanical	matic	mercurial
mechanism	melody	mercury
mechanist	melon	mercy
medal	melrose	mere
medalist	melt	merely
medallion	melted	merge
meddle	member	meridian
meddlesome	membership	merino
mediaeval	membrane	merit
medial	membran-	merited
medially	eous	meritorious
median	mememto	merkin
mediate	memoir	mermaid
mediation	memorable	merman
mediator	memorandum	merriment
mediatory	memorial	merriness
medical	memorial-	merry
medicament	ize	mersion
medicate	memorize	mesh
medication	memory	mesial
medicine	men	meslin
mediocrity	menace	mesmerism
meditate	menage	mess
meditation	menagerie	message
meditative	mend	messenger
medium	mendacious	messiah
medley	mender	messmate
meed	mendicant	messuage
meek	menhir	mestee
meekly	menial	met
meekness	meninges	metabasis
meeken	meningitis	metacentre
meerschaum	meniscus	metacism
meet	menology	metage
meeting	mental	metagenesis
megascope	mentally	metal
megrim	mention	metalepsis
melancholy	mentioned	metallic
melange	mentioning	metalline
melanizm	mentor	metallist
melanosis	menu	metallize
melanphyre	mephitic	metamor-
melée	mercantile	phic

metaphor	mighty	miniate
metaphy-	migniard	miniature
sics	migrate	minim
metaplasm	migration	minimize
metathesis	mild	minimized
metatome	mildew	minimum
mete	mile	minion
metempiric	mileage	minister
meteor	milestone	ministerial
meteoric	militant	ministering
meteorolite	military	ministration
meter	militate	ministry
method	militia	minium
methodical	milk	mink
methodist	milky	minor
methylene	mill	minority
metric	mill-dam	minstrel
metronome	millenary	mint
metropolis	millennial	minuet
metropo-	millennium	minus
litan	miller	minute
mettle	millet	minutely
mew	milliner	minuteness
mewl	millinery	minutiae
mezzo	million	minx
mezzotint	million-	miracle
miasm	aire	miraculous
mica	mill-stone	miradore
micado	millwright	mirage
mice	milsey	mirbane
mickle	mime	mire
microbe	mimesis	mirror
microcosm	mimetic	mirth
microphone	mimic	mirthful
microscope	minacious	miry
microzyme	minaret	misadventure
mid	mince	misalliance
midday	minced	misanthrope
middle	mincing	misapplica-
middle-age	mind	tion
midge	mindful	misapply
midget	mine	misappre-
midland	miner	ciated
midnight	mineral	misapprehend
midshipman	mineral-	misapprehen-
midst	ize	sion
midway	mineralogy	misappro-
mid-wife	minerva	priate
mien	minever	misarrange
might	mingle	misbecome

misbehave	misguided	mistress
misbelief	mishap	mistrust
misbeseem	misinform	misty
miscalcu-late	misjudge	misunder-stand
miscalcu-lation	mislaid	misunder-standing
miscarriage	mislay	misunder-stood
miscarry	mislead	
miscast	misled	misuse
miscellan-eous	mismanage	miswrite
miscellany	mismanage-ment	mite
mischance	misname	mitigate
mischarge	misogamist	mitre
mischief	misogyny	mitten
mischievous	mispersuade	mittimus
miscible	misplace	mix
misclaim	misprint	mixed
miscompute	misprise	mixture
misconceit	mispro-nounce	mizzen
misconceive	mispropor-tion	mizzen-top
misconsep-tion	misquote	mizzle
misconduct	misrate	mnemonics
misconstruc-tion	misreceive	moa
misconstrue	misrepre-sent	moan
miscounsel	misrepresen-tation	moaned
miscount	misrepute	moaning
miscreant	misrule	moat
misdeal	miss	mob
misdeed	missal	mobile
misdeem	missed	mobility
misdemean	misshapen	mobiliza-tion
misdemean-our	missile	mobolize
misdirect	missing	moble
misdoing	mission	moccasin
misdoubt	missionary	mock
mise	missive	mockery
miser	misspell	modalist
miserable	misspent	mode
misery	misstate	model
misfeasance	mist	moderate
misfit	mistake	moderation
misfortune	mistaken	modern
misgiving	mister	modernist
misgovern	mistletoe	modest
misguide	mistral	modesty
	mistranslate	modicum
		modifica-tion

modified	monitor	mop
modify	monitory	mope
modish	monitress	moraine
modulate	monk	moral
modulation	monkey	moralist
modus	monocar-	morality
mogul	dian	moralize
mohair	monichord	morass
mohammedan	monochrome	morbid
moil	monocracy	morbific
moist	monocrat	morbose
moisture	monodrama	morceau
molar	monogram	mordant
molasse	monograph	mordicant
mold	monolith	more
mole	monologue	moreen
molecule	monomania	morel
mole-hill	monomial	moreland
molest	monopathic	moreover
mollient	monopolize	morganatic
mollify	monopoly	morgue
moloch	monopteros	moribund
molten	monosyll-	morion
molto	able	morkin
mome	monotheist	mormon
moment	monotone	morn
momentary	monotonous	morning
moment-	monotony	morocco
arily	monsieur	morose
mementous	monsoon	morpheus
momentum	monster	morphew
monachal	monstrance	morphia
monad	monstrosity	morphosis
monandry	monstrous	morsel
monarch	montanic	mort
monarchal	montant	mortal
monarchy	monteith	mortality
monastery	month	mortar
monastic	monture	mortgage
monday	monument	mortgagee
monetary	mood	mortifi-
monetiza-	moody	or	cation
tion	moon	mortify
money	moonlight	mortise
moneyed	moonshine	mortmain
money-	moor	mortuary
order	or	mooring	mosaic
monger	moorland	mosque
mongrel	or	moose	mosquito
monism	or	moot	moss

moss-rose	moving	mump
mossy	mow	mumps
most	mows	munch
mostly	mower	mundane
mote	moxa	mundify
motet	moya	mundiva-
moth	mucchero	gant
mother	much	municipal
mother-in-	mucid	munifi-
law	mucilage	cence
motherless	mucous	munificent
motile	muculent	muniment
motion	mucus	munition
motionless	mucus-mem-	murage
motive	brane	mural
motley	mud	murder
motor	muddle	murderer
motor-boat	muddled	murderous
motor-car	muddy	murdress
motordrome	muff	muriatic
motor-	muffin	muricate
launch	muffle	murine
mottle	muffler	murk
mottled	mug	murky
motto	muggy	murmur
mould	mulatto	murrain
moulder	mulberry	murrion
mouldy	mule	muscat
moulinet	mull	muscle
moult	mullet	muscovado
moulting	mullion	muscular
mound	mulse	muse
mount	multeity	muser
mountain	multiform	musette
mounted	multiple	museum
mountain-	multipli-	mushroom
eer	cation	music
mountainous	multiplied	musical
mountebank	multiply	music-hall
mourn	multipotent	musician
mourner	multitude	musk
mournful	multitudi-	musket
mouse	nous	musketeer
mouser	multum	musketry
moustache	multure	musk-rose
mouth	mumble	musky
movable	mumm	muslin
move	mummer	musquash
movement	mummery	musquito
mover	mummy	musrole

muss	naiads	navigation
must	nail	navigator
mustard	naive	navvy
muster	naked	navy
musty	name	nay
mutability	nameless	naze
mutable	namely	neap
mutage	namesake	near
mute	nap	nearly
mutilate	nape	neat
mutilation	napery	nebula
mutinous	naptha	nebulous
mutiny	napkin	necessaries
mutter	napoleon	necessary
muttered	nappal	necessarily
mutual	narcotic	necessitate
mutually	narrate	necessity
muzzle	narration	neck
my	narrative	necklace
myalgia	narrow	necktie
mycology	nasal	necrology
myelites	nascal	necro-
myology	nasty	mancer
myopathy	nasute	necromancy
myope	natal	necropolis
myopy	natant	necrosis
myosis	nation	nectar
myosotis	national	need
myriad	nationality	needed
myriarch	native	needful
myriorama	nativity	needle
myrmidon	natron	needless
myrrh	natty	needlessly
myrtle	natural	needy
myself	naturalist	nefarious
mysis	naturalize	negation
mysterious	naturally	negative
mysteriously	nature	neglect
mystery	naught	neglectful
mystic	naughty	negligence
mystical	nausea	negligent
mystified	nauseous	negotiable
mystify	nautical	negotiate
myth	nautilus	negotiation
mythology	naval	negress
	nave	negresses
Nabit	navel	negro
nacre	navicular	negus
nadir	navigable	neigh
nag	navigate	neighbour

neighbour-	nibble	nix
hood	nibbler	-no
neighbourly	nice	nobility
neither	nicer	noble
nemesis	nicest	nobleman
nemorous	nicety	nobody
neogamist	niche	nocent
neophyte	nick	noctambu-
neoplastic	nickel	list
neoteric	nickname	noctograph
nepenthe	nictate	noctuary
nephalism	nidge	nocturnal
nephew	nidorous	nocturne
nephrite	nidulate	nod
nephritis	nidus	node
nepotism	niece	nodose
neptune	niggard	nodus
nervation	niggardly	noetic
nerve	nigger	nog
nervous	niggle	noils
nervous-	nigh	noise
ness	nigher	noisy
nescience	night	nomad
ness	nightfall	nomadic
nest	nightin-	nomancy
nestle	gale	nome
net	nightly	nomen-
nether	nightmare	clator
netting	night-watch	nominal
nettle	nigrescent	nominate
network	nihilism	nominated
neural	nihilist	nominative
neuralgia	nil	nominees
neurine	nimble	nomology
neurosis	nimbus	non-ability
neurotic	nimiety	nonchalant
neuter	nine	non-commiss-
neutral	ninefold	ioned
neutrality	nineteen	non-committal
néve	ninety	non-compli-
never	ninth	ance
nevertheless	nip	non-conduc-
new	nippers	tor
newel	nipple	non-content
newly	nisus	none
news	nitency	nonentity
newspaper	nitrate	non-essen-
newt	nitre	tial
next	nitrous	non-exist-
nib	niveous	ence

non-juror
non-obser-
    vance
nonpareil
nonplus
non-receipt
non-resi-
    dence
non-resident
non-resis-
    tant
nonsense
nonsensi-
    cal
non-solvent
non-toxis
nonsuit
nook
noon
noonday
noontide
noose
nor
norm
normal
norman
norse
north
northern
northman
northward
nose
nosegay
nosoco-
    mial
nosology
nostril
nostrum
not
notable
notary
notation
notch
note
noted
note-paper
nothing
notice
noticeable
noticed

notifica-
    tion
notify
notion
notoriety
notorious
notor-
    iously
notwith-
    standing
nougat
nought
noumenal
noumenon
noun
nourish
nourishment
nous
novation
novel
novelty
november
novice
novitiate
now
nowhere
nowise
noxious
nozzle
nubile
nuchal
nucleus
nude
nudge
nudged
nugatory
nugget
nuisance
null
nullity
numb
number
numberless
numeral
numerate
numerated
numeration
numerator
numerous
numerously

numisma-
    tist
nun
nuncio
nunnery
nuptial
nurse
nursery
nurture
nut
nutmeg
nutrient
nutrition
nutritive
nye
nymph
nystagmus

Oaf
oak
oaken
oar
oasis
oast
oat
oat-cake
oaten
oath
oat-meal
obcordate
obduce
obduction
obdurate
obedience
obedient
obeisance
obelisk
oberon
obese
obesity
obey
obfuscate
obit
obituary
object
objection
objectionable
objective
objurgate
oblate

oblation
obligate
obligation
obligatory
oblige
obligee
obliging
oblique
obliquity
obliterate
oblivion
oblivious
oblong
obloquy
obnoxious
obovate
obscene
obscure
obscurity
obsequious
observable
observant
observation
observe
obsidian
obsolete
obstacle
obstinate
obstrep-
  erous
obstruct
obstruc-
  tion
obstruent
obtain
obtainable
obtected
obtest
obtrude
obtrusive
obtuse
obtusion
obverse
obvert
obviate
obvious
occasion
occasioned
occasional
occasionally

occasionary
occident
occidental
occlude
occult
occupant
occupation
occupied
occupy
occur
occurred
occurrent
occurs
ocean
oceanic
ocellated
ochlesis
ochre
octagon
octant
octave
october
octofid
octogenary
octonary
ocular
odal
odd
odd-fellow
oddity
ode
odious
odium
odonto
odoriferous
odorous
odour
of
off
offal
offence
offend
offensive
offer
offered
offering
offertory
office
officer
official

officiate
officious
officious-
  ness
offing
offset
offspring
often
ogee
ogham
ogle
ogled
ogre
ogress
ohm
oil
oiled
oils
oily
ointment
old
older
oldest
oleate
oleon
olfactory
oligarchy
olitory
olivary
olive
oliver
olivet
olympia
ombre
omega
omelette
omen
ominous
omission
omit
omitted
omnibus
omniferous
omnipotent
omnipresent
omniscient
omoplate
omphacine
on,
once

one	oppose	organ
onerary	opposed	organic
onerous	opposite	organical
one's self	opposition	organism
onion	oppress	organist
onlooker	oppressed	organization
only	oppression	organize
onomancy	oppressive	organizer
onset	oppressor	organizing
onslaught	oppugn	organogen
onotology	oppugnant	orgies
onus	optative	orgues
onward	optic	oriel
onyx	optical	orient
oology	optigraph	oriental
ooze	optimism	orientate
opal	option	orifice
opalesce	optional	origin
opalescent	opulence	original
opaque	opulent	originate
open	opuscule	orillon
opened	or	orion
openly	oracle	orison
opera	oracular	orle
operant	oral	orlop
operate	orange	ornament
operation	oration	ornate
operator	orator	ornithic
operculum	oratory	ornithology
operetta	orb	orology
operose	orbate	orotund
opetide	orbiculate	orphan
ophicleide	orbit	orphrey
ophiolatry	orbital	orpin
ophite	orchard	orrery
opthalmia	orchestra	orthodox
opthalmic	orchestral	orthodoxly
opiane	orchid	orthodoxy
opiate	orchis	orthodromy
opificer	ord	orthoepy
opine	ordain	ortolan
opinion	ordeal	oscillate
opinionated	order	oscillation
opium	orderly	oscitant
oporice	ordinance	oscitate
oppilate	ordinary	osculant
opponent	ordinate	osculation
opportune	ordination	osier
opportuism	ordnance	osmose
opportunity	orgal	osprey

osseous	outrageous	overshadow
ossicle	outrage-	overshot
ossify	ously	oversight
ostensible	outrance	oversleep
ostent	outright	overslip
ostentation	outside	overstate
ostentatious	outsiders	overt
osteocope	outskirts	overtake
ostracism	outspoken	overthrow
ostrich	outstrip	overtime
otacoustic	outward	overtop
otaria	outwit	overture
other	outwork	overturn
otherwise	oval	overwhelm
otic	ovalbumen	ovine
otiose	ovary	oviparous
otology	ovate	oviposit
otto	ovation	ovoid
otter	oven	ovule
ottoman	over	ovum
oubliette	overact	owe
ouch	overalls	owes
ought	overawe	owing
ounce	overbalance	owl
ounces	overboard	own
our	overcast	owner
ourselves	overcharge	ox
oust	overcoat	oxalic
out	overcome	oxen
outbreak	overdo	oxide
outcast	overdone	oxidize
outcome	overdraw	oxygen
outcry	overdue	oxygon
outdo	overflow	oxyopia
outdoor	overflowing	oyer
outer	overhaul	oyster
outfit	overhead	ozone
outing	overheated	
outlandish	overjoyed	Pabular
outlaw	overland	pacation
outlay	overlay	pace
outlet	overlook	paced
outline	overmuch	pachyderm
outlive	overnight	pacific
outlook	overrake	pacioica-
outmost	overrate	tion
out-patient	overreach	pacify
outpost	overrun	pack
outpouring	oversea	package
outrage	overseer	packer

packet
pack-horse
packman
packing
pact
paction
pad
paddle
paddock
paddy
padella
padlock
paeans
pagan
paganism
page
pageant
pageantry
paginal
pagoda
pail
paillasse
pain
painful
painfully
painless
painlessly
pains-
    taking
paint
painter
painting
pair
pairing
palace
palanquin
palatable
palate
palatial
pale
paleaceous
paletot
palette
palfry
paling
palisade
pall
palladium
pallet
pallial

palliate
palliation
pallid
pallium
palm
palmate
palm-house
palmist
palpable
palpitate
palpitation
paltry
palsy
pampas
pamper
pamphlet
pan
panada
pancake
panch
pancratic
pandect
pandemon-
    ium
pander
pandora
pane
panegyric
panel
pang
panic
peniculate
panivorous
pannade
pannel
pannier
panoply
panorama
panoramic
pansy
pant
pantaloon
pantheism
panther
pantile
pantler
pantograph
pantology
pantomime
panton

pantry
pap
papacy
papal
paper
paper-
    hangers
papist
papoose
pappose
papulous
papyrus
par
parable
parachute
paraclete
parade
paradigm
paradise *
paradox *
paradox *
paraffin
paragenic
paragoge
paragon
paragraph *
parallax
parallel
paralogy
paralysis
paralyze
paramount
paramoun
parapet *
parapher-
    nalia
paraphrase
parasite*
parasol
paratnesis
parboil
parcel
parcenary
parch
parchment
pard
pare
parent
parental
parenthesis

*In these outlines R may safely be indicated.

parenticide	passade	patter
parget	passage	pattern
parietal	pass-book	patty
parish	passed	paucity
park	passenger	pauper
parley	passer-by	pause
parliament	passing	pave
parlour	passion	pavement
parochial	passionate	pavilion
parody	passion-	paw
parole	ately	pawl
paronomasia	passioned	pawn
parotis	passive	pax
parquetry	passports	pay
parricide	past	payable
parrot	paste	pay-bill
parse	pastel	pay-day
parsee	pastil	payed
parsimony	pastime	payee
parson	pastor	paymaster
part	pastoral	payment
partake	pastry	pea
parted	pasture	peace
parterre	pasty	peaceful
partial	pat	peacefully
partiality	patch	peace-
participate	paten	maker
participation	patent	peach
participle	patented	peacock
particle	patentee	peahen
particular	paternal	peak
particularly	paternity	peaky
particularity	path	peal
particulars	pathetic	peanut
parting	pathless	pear
partisan	pathology	pearl
partition	pathos	pearly
partlet	pathway	peasant
partly	patience	pease
partner	patient	peat
partnership	patiently	pebble
partook	patois	peccable
partridge	patriarch	peck
party	patrician	pectic
parvenu	patrimony	pectinate
paschal	patriot	pectorial
pasigraphy	patriotism	peculate
pasquin	patrol	peculation
pass	patronizes	peculiar
passable	patten	peculiarity

pecuniary	penetrate	percuss
ped	penetra-	percussion
pedagogue	tion	perdition
pedal	penetrative	perdu
pedant	peninsula	peregrine
pedantic	peninsu-	peremptory
pedate	late	perennial
peddle	penitence	pererration
peddler	penitent	perfect
pedestal	penitential	perfectly
pedestrian	penknife	perfection
pedigree	penman	perficient
pediment	penmanship	perfidious
peel	pennant	perfidy
peep	pennate	perforate
peer	penniless	perforation
peerage	penny	perforce
peeress	penology	perform
peerless	pensile	performance
peevish	pension	performer
peg	pensive	perfume
peg-top	pent	perfumery
peirastic	pentacle	perfunc-
pelagian	pentagon	tory
pelerene	pentaspast	perhaps
pelf	pentateuch	peri
pelican	pentecost	perianth
pelisse	pente-	pericarp
pell	costal	pericope
pellet	pentile	peril
pellucid	penult	perilous
pelt	penurious	period
pelted	penury	periodic
peltate	peony	periodical
peltry	people	peripa-
pelvis	pepper	tetic
pemmican	pepsine	periphery
pen	peptic	peripteral
penal	peracute	periptery
penalty	peradven-	periscope
penance	ture	perish
penates	perambulate	perishable
pence	perceive	peristaltic
pencil	percent	periton-
pendant	percentage	itis
pendent	perceptible	perjure
pending	perch	perk
pendulous	perchance	permanence
pendulum	percipient	permanent
penetrable	percolate	permanently

permeable
permeate
permeation
permiscible
permissible
permission
permit
permutable
permutation
pernicious
perone
perorate
peroration
peroxide
perpend
perpendic-
    ular
perpetrate
perpetra-
    tion
perpetual
perpetuate
perpetuity
perplex
perplexing
perplexity
perquisite
perquisition
perron
perry
persecute
persecution
persever-
    ance
persevere
persevered
persian
persiflage
persist
persistence
persistent
person
personage
personal
personality
personate
personation
personifi-
    cation
personified

personify
perspective
perspica-
    cious
perspicuity
perspiration
perspire
persuade
persuasion
persuasive
pert
pertain
pertinacious
pertinacity
perturb
perturbation
pertuse
pertusion
peruke
perusal
peruse
pervade
pervasion
perverse
perversion
pervert
pervesti-
    gate
pervious
pesade
pesky
pessimist
pessimistic
pest
pester
pestering
pestilent
pestle
pet
petal
petard
petition
petrify
petroleum
petronel
petted
petticoat
petty
petulance
petulant

peuce
pew
pewter
phalanks
phantas-
    cope
phantasm
phantastic
phantasy
phantom
pharisee
pharmacology
pharmaco-
    poeia
pharmacy
phase
pheasant
phenomenal
phenomenon
philander
philanthro-
    pic
philanthro-
    pist
philanthropy
philatelist
philhar-
    monic
philology
philospher
philoso-
    phical
philosophy
philter
phlebology
phlegm
phlegmatic
phlox
phocal
phoenix
phonetic
phonograph
phonog-
    rapher
phonography
phonology
phonotype
phosphor
phospho-
    rate

phosphor-	piece	piquet
escence	pied	pirate
phosphorous	pier	piscary
photo	pierce	pissasphalt
photograph	pierced	piste
photology	piercing	pistil
photopsy	pietist	pistol
phrase	piety	pit
phraseogram	pig	pitch
phraseo-	pig-headed	pitcher
graphy	pigeon	pitecus
phraseology	pigment	pith
phrenitis	pigmy	pithy
phrenolo-	pigtail	pitiful
gist	pike	pitiless
phrenology	pilaster	pity
phrensy	pile	pivot
phthisis	pilgrim	pix
phylactery	pilgrimage	pixy
phylarchy	pill	placable
phylogeny	pillage	placard
physic	pillar	place
physical	pillion	placed
physician	pillory	places
physics	pillow	placid
physiognomy	pilot	plafond
physiology	pimple	plagiary
physique *	pin	plague
piacular	pinafore	plaice
pianette	pinaster	plaid
piano	pincers	plain
piazza	pinch	plainer
pibroch	pine	plainness
pica	pine-apple	plaint
picador	pinery	plaintiff
picaroon	pinion	plaintive
piccadilly	pink	plait
piccage	pinnace	plaiter
piccolo	pinnacle	plan
pick	pinnate	planch
pickaxe	pint	planchet
picked	pioneer	plane
pickle	pious	planet
picnic	pip	plank
picrine	pipe	planner
pictorial	piper	plant
picture	pippin	plantain
pictur-	piquancy	plantation
esque	piquant	planter
pie	pique	plaque

* The dot is used to distinguish from physic.

plash	plethora	poach
plass	pleura	poacher
plaster	pleural	pocket
plastic	pleurisy	pocket-book
plastron	plevin	pocket-hole
plat	plexus	pod
plate	pliable	podagral
plateau	pliancy	podium
platen	pliant	poem
plate-rack	plica	poesy
platform	plicate	poet
platinum	pliers	poetic
platonic	plight	poetical
platoon	plights	poetry
platter	plinth	poignant
plaudit	pliocene	point
plausible	plod	pointed
play	plodder	poise
player	plodding	poison
playful	plot	poisoning
play-house	plotted	poisonous
playing	plotter	poke
playmate	plotting	poker
plaything	plough	polar
play-wright	ploughing	polarity
plea	plough-	polders
pleach	share	pole
plead	plover	pole-axe
pleaded	pluck	polemic
pleader	plucked	police
pleading	plucky	policy
pleasant	plug	polish
please	plum	polished
pleased	plumbago	polisher
pleasurable	plumber	polite
pleasure	plumb-line	political
plebeian	plume	politician
plebiscite	plummet	polka
pledge	plump	poll
plenary	plunge	pollard
plenarty	plunket	pollen
pleni-	pluperfect	pollicita-
lunar	plural	tion
plenipoten-	plus	poll-tax
tiaries	plush	pollute
plenist	plutonic	polluted
plenteous	pluvial	pollution
plentiful	ply	pollux
plenty	pneumatic	polo
pleonastic	pneumonia	poltroon

polverine
polyarchy
polygamy*
polyglot*
polygon*
polygram
polygraph
polyphonic
polypus
polyscope
polysyllable
polytechnic
polytheism
polytype
pomace
pommel
pomology
pomposity
pompous
poncho
pond
ponder
ponderous
poniard
pontage
pontee
pontiff
pontifice
pontificial
pontoon
pony
pooh
pool
poop
poor
poorer
poorest
pop
pope
popery
popish
poplar
poplin
poppet
poppy
popular
popularity
populate
population
populous

porcate
porcelain
porch
porcine
pore
pork
porotic
porous
porphyry
porrect
porridge
porringer
port
portable
portal
portcullis
portend
portent
portentous
porter
portfolio
portgrave
port-hole
portico
portion
portlast
portly
portman-
teau
portmote
portrait
portray
portrayal
pose
posit
position
positive
possess
possession
possessor
posset
possibil-
ities
possible
post
postage
postal
post-card
post-date
poster

posterior
posterity
postern
posthumous
postil
postillate
postillion
posting
postman
postmaster
post-mortem
post-note
post-office
postpone
postponed
postscript
posture
posy
pot
potash
potato
potence
potent
potentate
potential
pother
pot-hook
potion
pot-pourri
pottage
potter
pottery
pottle
potulent
pouch
poultice
poultry
pounce
pounced
pound
poundage
pounder
pour
pouring
poussette
pout
pouter
poverty
powder
powdered

* In these outlines insert the E vowel for ease.

powder-	precise	prelect
magazine	precision	preliminary
power	preclude	prelude
powerful	precocious	premature
pox	precogitate	premeditate
praam	precognition	premier
practical	precompose	premium
practice	preconceive	premonition
practising	precondemn	premotion
practitioner	preconsign	premunition
praecipe	precontract	prenomen
pragmatic	precursor	prenominate
prairie	predaceous	preoccupy
praise	predecease	preoption
praised	predecessor	preordain
prakrit	predesign	prepaid
prance	predestinate	preparation
prank	predestination	preparatory
prate	predicament	prepare
pratique	predicate	prepared
prattle	predict	prepay
pravity	prediction	prepayment
prawn	predilection	prepense
praxis	predispose	prepon-
pray	predominant	derate
prayer	predominate	preposition
preach	pre-eminent	prepositor
preacher	pre-emption	prepossess
preachment	preen	preposterous
preadmonish	pre-engagement	prepotent
preamble	pre-establish	preremote
prebend	pre-examine	prerogative
precarious	pre-exist	presage
precaution	preface	presbyter
precautionary	prefer	presbyterian
precautious	preferable	presbytery
precede	preference	prescient
precedence	preferment	prescind
preceding	prefix	prescribe
precedent	prefulgency	prescript
precentor	pregnable	prescription
precept	pregnant	presence
precession	prehensile	present
precinct	prehistoric	presentable
precious	prejudge	presentation
precipice	prejudicate	presentiment
precipitant	prejudice	presently
precipitate	prejudiced	preserve
precipitous	prelacy	preserver
précis	prelate	preses

preside	prickle	privative
president	prickly	privilege
presidential	pride	privy
press	prided	prize
pressed	prier	prized
pressing	priest	probability
pressman	priestcraft	probable
press-room	priestess	probate
pressure	priesthood	probation
prestation	priestly	probation-
prestige	prig	ary
presume	prim	probe
presumed	primacy	probity
presumedly	prima	problem
presumption	donna	proboscis
presumptive	primarily	procacious
presump-	primary	procedure
tuous	primate	proceed
pretences	prime	proceeded
pretend	primer	proceeding
pretender	primeval	proceeds
pretension	priming	process
pretentious	primitive	procession
preter-	primo	prochein
lapsed	primogenial	procinct
preter-	primrose	proclaim
mission	primula	proclama-
pretermit	primus	tion
preter-	prince	proclivity
natural	princely	procrasti-
pretext	princess	nation
pretorian	principal	procreate
prettiest	princi-	procreation
pretty	pality	procrustean
prevail	principle	proctor
prevalence	print	procurator
prevalent	printed	procure
prevaricate	printer	procured
prevent	printing	prod
preventa-	prior	prodigal
tive	priory	prodigious
prevention	prise	prodigy
preventive	prism	produce
previous	prismatic	produced
previously	prison	product
prevision	prisoner	production
prey	pristine	productive
price	privacy	proem
priceless	private	profanation
prick	privation	profane

profanity	promising	proposal
profess	promontory	proposes
professed	promote	proposition
profession	promoter	propound
professional	promotion	proprietor
professor	prompt	propulsion
proffer	prompted	propylon
proficient	prompter	prore
profile	promptitude	prorector
profit	promptly	prorecep-
profitable	promptness	tion
profligate	promulgate	prorogation
profound	promulga-	prorogue
profundity	tion	proruption
profuse	pronaos	prosaic
profusion	pronation	proscribe
prog	prone	proscrip-
progenitor	prong	tion
progeny	pronoun	prose
prognosis	pronounce	prosecute
prognostic	pronounced	prosecuting
programme	pronuncia-	prosecutor
progress	tion	proselyte
progression	proof	proser
progressive	prop	proslavery
prohibit	propa-	prosody
project	ganda	prospect
projection	propagate	prospective
projet	propagation	prospectus
prolate	propel	prosper
proletar-	propeller	prosperity
ian	propend	prosperous
prolicide	propense	prostate
prolific	propensity	prostitute
prolix	proper	prostrate
prolocutor	properly	prostration
prologue	property	prosy
prolong	prophecy	protatic
prolonga-	prophet	protect
tion	prophetic	protection
prolusion	propination	protective
promenade	propitiate	protector
prominence	propitiation	protector-
prominent	propitious	ate
promin-	proplasm	protend
ently	propolis	protervity
promiscuous	proportion	protest
promise	propor-	protestant
promised	tional	protesta-
promises	proportionate	tion

protest-ingly	prudent	puissant
prothesis	prudential	puke
protocol	prudery	pule
protogenic	prudish	pull
protomartyr	prune	pullet
protoplasm	pruner	pulley
prototype	prurient	pullman
protract	pry	pulp
protracted	psalm	pulpit
protraction	psalmist	pulsate
protrac-tor	psalmody	pulse
	psalter	pulverize
protrude	pseudo-blepsis	pulvil
protrusion	pseudograph	puma
protuberated	pseudonym	pumicate
proud	psilanthro-pist	pumice
provable		pump
prove	psora	pumpkin
provection	psyche	pun *
proven	psychic	punch
provender	psycho-logical	puncheon
proverb		punctilious
proverbial	pterygoid	punctual
provide	ptyalism	punctually
provided	puberty	punctuate
providen-tial	public	punctuation
	publicly	puncture
province	publican	pungent
provincial	publication	punish
provine	publicity	punishable
provision	publish	purchase
provisional	publisher	purchased
provision-ary	puck	purchasing
	pucker	pure
provisor	pudder	purgation
provisory	pudding	purgative
provocation	puddle	purgatory
provocative	puerile	purge
provoke	puff	purification
provost	puffer	purify
prow	puffin	purist
prowess	puffy	puritan
prowl	pug	purity
proximate	pug-dog	purl
proxime	pugil	purloin
proxy	pugilism	purloined
prude	pugilist	purparty
prudence	pugilistic	purple
prudency	pugnacious	purport
		purpose

* See Preface, but note that these outlines are safe.

purposeless	quadrant	quench
purr	quadrat	quenchless
purse	quadrate	querent
purser	quadratic	querist
pursuant	quadriga	queried
pursue	quadrille	querl
pursuit	quadrill-	quern
purulent	ion	querulous
purvey	quadruped	query
purveyance	quadruple	quest
purveyor	quaestor	question
purview	quaggy	queue
pus	quagmire	quib
push	quail	quibble
pusilla-	quaint	quibbler
nimity	quake	quick
puss	quaker	quicken
pustilate	quaky	quicklime
put	qualification	quickly
puteal	qualify	quicksand
putid	qualities	quiddity
putres-	quality	quiesce
cence	qualm	quiescent
putrid	qualmish	quiet
puttock	quandary	quietude
putty	quantity	quietus
puzzle	quarantine	quill
puzzled	quarrel	quilt
pyjamas	quarreling	quilted
pygmy	quarrelsome	quince
pylorus	quarry	quinine
pyramid	quart	quinsy
pyre	quarter	quint
pyretic	quarter-day	quintal
pyrexia	quarter-	quintan
pyrolatory	deck	quintes-
pyrologist	quarterly	sence
pyrology	quarter-	quintet
pyromania	master	quip
pyrope	quartern	quire
pyrophorus	quartette	quirk
pyrosis	quarto	quit
python	quartz	quite
pyx	quash	quittal
	quaver	quiver
Quab	quay	qui-vive
quack	queen	quiz
quackery	queenly	quod
quadra	queer	quodlibet
quadrangle	quell	quoiffure

quoin	railway	rapidly
quoit	raiment	rapier
quotation	rain	rapine
quote	rainbow	rappel
quoted	rainy	rapport
quoter	raise	rapt
quoth	rake	rapture
quotient	raking	rare
	rakish	rarely
Rabate	rale	rarity
rabbet	ralliance	rascal
rabbi	rally	rase
rabbit	ram	rash
rabble or	ramble	rasher
rabid	rambling	rasp
race	rameous	raspberry
raceme	ramifica-	rasure
racer	tion	rat
rach	ramify	ratch
racial	ramous	ratchet
racing	ramp	ratchil
rack	rampage	rate
racket	rampant	rather
racy	rampart	ratify
radial	ramshakle	ratio
radiance	ramskin	ration
radiant	ramulous	rational
radiate	ran	rationalist
radiation	ranch	ratlin
radical	ranchman	ratten
radicate	rancid	ratter
radish	rancour or	rattle
radium	rand	rattled
radix	random	raucous
raff	rang	ravage
raffle	range	rave
raft	ranger	raven
rafter	rank	ravenous
rag	rankle	ravenously
rage	ransack	ravine
ragged	ransom or	ravish
raging	rant	ravishment
ragman	ranter	raw
ragout	rap	ray
raid	rapacious	rayless
rail	rapacity	raze
railing	rape	razor
raillery	raphaelite	razzle
railroad	rapid	reabsorb

reach	recant	recommenda-
reached	recapitulate	tion
react	recapture	recommended
reaction	recede	recommit
read	receipt	recompense
readable	receive	recompile
readers	received	recompose
readily	receiver	reconcile
reading	receiving	reconcilia-
readjust	recent	tion
ready	recently	recondense
ready-made	receptacle	recondite
ready-	recepti-	reconfirm
money	bility	reconnoitre
reaffirm	reception	reconquer
real	receptive	reconquest
realism	recess	reconsider
realist	recesses	reconsid-
realistic	recharge	eration
reality	recheat	reconstruct
realization	recipe	reconvey
realize	recipient	record
really	reciprocal	recorded
realm	reciprocate	recoup
ream	recision	recover
reap	recital	recoverable
reaper	recitation	recovery
reappear	recite	recreant
rear	reckless	recreat
rearrange	reckon	recreation
rearward	reclaim	recrimina-
reascend	reclaimant	tion
reason	reclamation	recruit
reasonable	recline	rectangle
reassert	reclined	rectify
reassure	recluse	rectitude
reaver	reclusion	rector
rebate	recognisable	rectory
rebel	recogni-	rectum
rebelled	sance	recumbent
rebellion	recognise	recuperate
rebellious	recognised	recur
rebound	recognition	recurrence
rebuff	recoil	recurrent
rebuke	recoin	recurvate
rebus	recollect	recusant
rebut	recollec-	red
recalcit-	tion	redact
rant	recommence	redan
recall	recommend	redden

reddition	refiner	regenerate
redeem	refit	regeneration
redeemable	reflect	regent
redeemer	reflected	regicide
redelivery	reflection	regime
redemand	reflector	regiment
redemise	reflex	regimental
redemption	reflux	region
red-hot	reform	register
redirection	reformation	registered
red-lead	reforma-	registrar
red-letter	tory	registration
redolence	reformed	registry
redolent	reformer	reglet
redoubt	refract	regnant
redoubtable	refraction	regrate
redoubted	refractory	regrater
redound	refragable	regress
redraw	refrain	regression
redress	refrained	regret
reduce	refrangible	regretted
reduced	refreshed	regular
reducible	refresh-	regularly
reduct	ment	regularity
reduction	refrigerate	regulations
redundant	refriger-	regulus
reed	ator	rehabili-
reeded	refuge	tate
re-edify	refugee	rehabili-
reef	refulgent	tation
reek	refund	rehearsal
reeky	refunded	rehearse
reel	refusal	rehearsed
re-elect	refuse	rehearsing
reeming	refused	reigle
re-enact	refusing	reign
re-enforce	refutation	reigning
re-enter	refute	reimbody
re-establish	regain	reimburse
reeve	regained	rein
re-examine	regal	reinstate
re-export	regale	reinstate-
refectory	regalia	ment
refer	regality	reiterate
referee	regard	reiteration
reference	regarded	reject
referen-	regardless	rejection
tial	regatta	rejoice
refine	regelation	rejoiced
refinement	regency	rejoicing

rejoin	remedial	renewed
rejoinder	remedy	renewing
rejoint	remember	renitent
rejuvenate	remembered	rennet
rekindle	remembrance	renounce
relapse	remigrate	renovate
relate	remind	renovation
related	reminded	renown
relating	reminder	rent
relation	reminis-	rentable
relative	cences	rental
relax	reminiscent	renter
relaxation	remise	renuncia-
relay	remiss	tion
release	remission	re-open
relegate	remissive	re-opened
relent	remit	reorgani-
relentless	remittal	zation
relet	remittance	reorganize
relevance	remnant	repack
relevant	remodel	repaid
reliability	remon-	repair
reliable	strance	repaired
reliance	remon-	repairing
reliant	strant	repairer
relic	remonstrate	reparable
relief	remorse	reparation
relieve	remorseful	reparative
relieved	remote	repartee
relight	remould	or repass
religion	remount	repast
religiosity	removal	repay
religious	remove	repeal
relinquish	remuner-	repeat
relique	able	repeated
relish	remuneration	repeater
relucent	remunera-	repel
reluctance	tive	repellent
reluctant	renais-	repent
reluctant-	sance	repentance
ly	renal	repentant
rely	renascent	repercuss
remain	reencoun-	repertoire
remainder	ter	repetition
remaining	rend	repine
remand	render	replace
remanent	rendezvous	replenish
remark	renegade	replete
remarkable	renew	repletion
remediable	renewal	replied

reply	reputation	resoluble
report	repute	resolute
reporter	request	resolution
reporting	requiem	resolve
repose	require	resolvent
reposit	requirement	resonant
repossess	requisite	resort
repoussé	requisition	resound
reprehend	requisitive	resource
reprehen- sible	requital	respect
reprehension	requite	respecta- bility
represent	reread	respectable
represen- tation	reredos	respective
	rescind	respectively
	rescript	respersion
represen- tative	rescription	respirable
	rescue	respiration
repress	rescuer	respire
repression	research	respite
repressive	reseat	resplendent
reprieve	resection	respond
reprimand	resem- blance	response
repri- manded	resemble	responsi- bility
reprint	resent	responsible
reprisal	resented	responsive
reprise	resentment	rest
reproach	reservation	restaurant
reproachable	reserve	restem
reprobate	reservist	restful
reprobation	reset	restfulness
reproduce	resettlement	resting- place
reproduction	resiant	restitution
reproof	reside	restive
reprovable	residence	restless
reproval	resident	restlessness
reprove	residential	restoration
reptation	residue	restore
reptile	resign	restrain
republic	resignation	restrainable
republican	resigned	restraint
republica- tion	resile	restrict
republish	resiliency	restriction
repudiate	resin	restrictive
repudiation	resinous	restringent
repugnant	resipis- cence	result
repulse	resist	resume
repulsion	resistance	resumption
reputable	resistible	

resupina-	revel	rhomb
tion	revelation	rhubarb
resurrection	revenge	rhumb
resusci-	reverberate	rhyme
table	revere	rhythm
resuscitate	reverence	riant
retail	reverend	rib
retain	reverent	ribald
retained	reverently	rice
retainer	reverse	rich
retake	reversed	richest
retaliate	reversing	riches
retaliation	reversion	rick
retard	revest	rickets
retch	review	rickety
retent	revile	rid
retention	reviling	riddance
reticence	reviler	riddle
reticule	revisal	riddling
retina	revise	ride
retinue	revised	rideau
retire	revising	rider
retirement	revision	ridge
retort	revisit	ridicule
retorted	revival	ridiculous
retouch	revivalist	riding
retract	revive	ridotto
retraction	revocable	rife
retreat	revocation	rifle
retrench	revoke	rifled
retrench-	revoked	rift
ment	revolt	rig
retribution	revolution	rigation
retriev-	revolu-	rigger
able	tionary	rigging
retrieve	revolve	right
retroact	revolver	rightly
retroaction	revulsion	righteous
retrocede	reward	righteous-
retrocession	rewarded	ness
retrograde	rewarder	rigid
retrospect	rewrite	rigidity
retrospec-	rex	riglet
tion	rhapsody	rigol
return	rheometry	rigorous
retuse	rhetoric	rigour
reunion	rheumatic	rile
reveal	rheumatism	rill
revealed	rhinoceros	rim
revealing	rhodium	rime

rimous	roborant	rosicru-
rimple	robust	cian
rind	roc	rosin
rindle	rochet	rosland
ring	rock	rostel
ringlet	rocker	roster
rink	rockery	rostrum
riot	rocket	rosy
rioting	rocky	rot
riotous	rod	rota
rip	rode	rotary
ripe	rodent	rotate
ripen	rodomont	rotation
ripple	roe	rote
rippling	rogation	rotten
ript	rogue	rotund
rise	roguery	rotundity
risen	roll	roué
riser	role	rouge
risible	roll	rough
rising	rolled	roulette
risk	roller	round
risky	rolling	roundabout
rissole	roman	rounder
rite	romance	roundness
ritual	romanic	rouse
ritualism	romantic	roused
rival	romp	rousing
rivalry	rondeau	rout
rive	rondle	routed
rivel	rood	route
riven	roof	routine
river	rook	roux
rivet	rookery	rove
rivose	room	row
rivulet	roomy	rowdy
rixation	roop	rowel
road	roost	royal
roadway	rooster	royalism
roam	root	royalist
roan	ropalic	royalty
roar	rope	rub
roared	roric	rubbed
roaring	rosary	rubber
roast	roscid	rubbish
roaster	rose	rubble
rob	roseal	rubefa-
robbery	roseate	cient
robe	rosemary	rubescent
robin	rosette	rubicund

ruble
rubric
ruby
ruck
ructation
rudder
ruddle
ruddy
rude
rudiment
rudimental
rue
ruff
ruffian
ruffle
ruffled
rufous
rug
rugate
rugged
ruin
ruination
ruinous
rule
rum
rumble
rumbling
ruminant*
ruminate *
rumination*
rummage *
rumour
rump
rumple *
run
rune
rung
runic
runnel *
runner
running *
runt
ruption
rupture
rural
ruse
rush
rushed
rusk
russet

russian
rust
rustic
rusticate
rusticity
rustle
rusty
rut
ruth
ruthless
rutilant
rye
ryot

Sabaoth
sabbath
sabbatic
sabianism
sabine
sable
sabot
sabre
sabulosity
sacbut
saccharine
saccular
sacerdotal
sack
sackage
sackcloth
sackful
sacking
sacrament
sacramental
sacred
sacrificial
sacrifice
sacrificed
sacrilege
sacrile-
 gious
sacrist
sacristan
sad
sadder
sadden
sadly
saddle
saddled
saddler

sadducee
safe
safely
safeness
safeguard
safety
saffron
sag
sagacious
sagacity
sage
sagittal
sago
sail
sailable
sailor
sail-yard
saint
sainted
saintly
sake
salad
salary
sale
saleable
salebros-
 ity
salebrous
salesman
salic
salient
saline
salique
saliva
sallet
sallow
sally
salmon
saloon
salop
salt
saltation
salter
saltpetre
salubrious
salutary
salutation
salute
salvage
salvation

* The vowel may be written to either consonant.

salve	sash	scalene
salver	sat	scall
salvo	satan	scallop
same	satanic	scalp
sameness	satchel	scaly
sample	sate	scamp
sampler	sateen	scamper
sanable	satiate	scan
sanative	satiety	scandal
sanatorium	satin	scandalous
sanatory	satire	scanned
sanctifi-	satirical	scant
cation	satisfaction	scanty
sanctify	satisfactory	scape
sancti-	satisfy	scape-goat
monious	satisfying	scapement
sanction	sative	scar
sanctioned	saturate	scarce
sanctioning	saturday	scarcely
sanctuary	satyr	scare
sand	sauce	scared
sandal	saucepan	scarf
sand-bag	saucer	scarious
sand-paper	saucisse	scarlet
sandwich	saucy	scarp
sandy	saunter	scathe
sane	sausage	scatter
song	savage	scattered
sanguine	savagey	scavenger
sanitation	savant	scene
sanity	save	scenery
sank	saving	scenic
sanscrit	saviour	scent
sap	savory	scentless
sapient	savour	sceptic
sapless	savoury	sceptical
sapling	savoy	sceptre
saponaceous	saw	schedule
saporific	saxatile	scheme
sapphire	say	schemer
sarcasm	saying	schesis
sarcastic	scabs	schism
sarcenet	scabbard	schist
sarcology	scabious	scholar
sarcoph-	scad	scholarship
agus	scaffold	school
sardine	scalade	school-board
sardius	scald	school-
sardonic	scalded	fellow
sartorial	scale	schooling

school-	scrag	seal
master	scramble	sealing
school-	scrambled	seam
mistress	scrap	seance
schooner	scrape	sear
sciagraph	scraper	search
sciatica	scratch	searchable
science	scratches	searcher
scientific	scrawl	searching
scientist	screak	searchlight
scilicet)	scream	season
scimitar	screamed	seasonable
scintilla-	screech	seat
tion	screed	seaward
sciolism	screen	sebaceous
scion	screw	secant
scioptic	scribble	secede
scirrhus	scribbled	seclude
scissel	scribe	seclusion
scission	scrimmage	second
scissors	scrimp	secondary
sclerotic	scrip	secrecy
scobs	script	secret
scoff	scriptual	secretarial
scoffer	scripture	secretari-
scoffing	scrivener	ship
scold	scrofula	secretary
sconce	scrog	secrete
scone	scroll	secretion
scope	scrub	secretly
scorch	scrubbed	sect
scorching	scruple	sectary
score	scrupulous	section
scoria	scrutinize	sectional
scorn	scrutiny	sector
scornful	scud	secular
scornfully	souffle	secularity
scorpion	scull	secure
scot	scullery	security
scotch	sculptor	sedate
scotchman	sculpture	sedative
scotia	scum	sedent
scotomy	scumble	sedge
scoundrel	scurf	sedition
scourge	scurrilous	seduce
scourged	scut	seduction
scout	scutage	seductive
scow	scuttle	sedulous
scowl	scythe	see
scrabble	sea	seed

seeded	self-love	sensuous
seedling	self-made	sent
seedsman	self-pos-	sentence
seeing	sessed	sentenced
seek	self-praise	sentential
seeker	self-reli-	sententious
seel	-ance	sentient
seem	self-respect	sentiment
seeming	self-sacri-	sentimental
seemingly	fice	sentinel
seemly	sell	sentry
seen	selvedge	sepal
seer	semaphore	separable
seethe	semblance	separate
segment	semblant	separates
segno	semeio-	separation
segregate	graphy	separator
seine	semen	sepia
seismal	semencine	sepiment
seismograph	semi	sepoy
seize	semibreve	sept
seized	seminal	september
seizure	seminary	septenary
seldom	semiquaver	septic
select	semitic	sepulchre
selected	semitone	sequacious
selection	semolina	sequel
self	semplice	sequence
self-	senary	sequester
abasement	senate	sequestrate
self-	senator	seraph
centred	send	seraphic
self-command	senescence	sere
self-conceit	seneschal	serenade
self-congratu-	senile	serena
lation	senior	serenity
self-congratu-	senna	serf
latory	senocular	serge
self-	sensation	sergeant
conscious	sensational	serial
self-	sense	seriate
contained	senseless	series
self-control	sensibility	serious
self-denial	sensible	seriousness
self-esteem	sensibly	sermon
self-grati-	sensitive	serosity
fication	sensorial	serpent
self-govern-	sensual	serration
ment	sensualist	serried
selfish	sensuality	serrulate

serum	shady	shelf
servant	shaft	shell
serve	shag	shelter
served	shaggy	shelve
server	shagreen	shepherd
service	shake	shepherdess
serviceable	shaken	sherbet
serviette	shakes-	sherd
servile	pearian	sheriff
servitor	shaky	sherry
servitude	shale	shew
sesame	shall	shewed
session	shallot	shield
set	shallow	shift
setaceous	shalt	shilling
set-down	sham	shimmer
set-off	shaman	shin
seton	shamble	shine
settee	shame	shingle
setting	shameless	shiny
settle	shampoo	ship
settlement	shamrock	shipmate
settler	shank	shipment
settling	shape	shipping
seven	shard	shipwreck
seventeen	share	shire
seventh	shareholder	shirk
seventy	shark	shirked
sever	sharp	shirt
several	sharpen	shiver
severe	sharpened	shoal
severed	sharper	shoat
severity	shatter	shock
sew	shave	shod
sewer	shaving	shoddy
sex	shawl	shoe
sexagenary	she	shoes
sexless	sheaf	shone
sextain	shear	shook
sextant	sheath	shoot
sextile	sheave	shop
sexton	shed	shopman
sexual	shedding	shore
shabbily	sheen	shoreless
shabby	sheep	shorn
shack	sheepish	short
shackle	sheer	shortbread
shade	sheet	shorten
shadow	shekel	shortest
shadowy	shekinah	shorthand

shortly	sickly	silvery
shortness	sickness	simial
shot	side	similar
should	side-board	similarity
shoulder	side-light	simile
shout	sidelong	similitude
shouted	sideral	simious
shove	sidero-	simmer
shovel	graphy	simony
shoveller	sidesman	simoon
show	sidewalk	simper
show-case	siding	simple
shower	sidle	simple-
showery	siege	minded
showman	siesta	simplest
shown	sieve	simpleton
showy	sift	simplicity
shrank	sigh	simplify
shrapnel	sighed	simply
shrewd	sight	simulate
shriek	sightless	simulation
shrieked	sign	simulta-
shrift	signal	neous
shrill	signature	sin
shrimp	signet	sinapis
shrine	significance	since
shrink	significent	sincere
shrive	signified	sincerity
shrivel	signifies	sine
shroud	signify	sinecure
shrub	sign-post	sinew
shrubbery	sikh	sinful
shrug	silence	sing
shrunk	silent	singer
shudder	silently	singing
shuffle	silex	single
shuffler	silhouette	single-
shun	silhouetted	handed
shunt	silicate	singular
shut	silicon	singularity
shutter	siliqua	sinister
shuttle	silk	sinistrous
shy	silken	sink
sibilant	silky	sinking
sibilation	sill	sinless
siccation	sillon	sinner
siccity	silly	sinology
sick	silt	sinopia
sicken	silurian	sinople
sickle	silver	sinter

sinuate	skirt	slept
sinuation	skit	slice
sinuosity	skiver	slick
sip	skulk	slid
siphon	skull	slide
sir	skurry	slight
sire	sky	slightly
siren	skyward	slim
sirius	slab	slime
sirloin	slack	slimy
sirocco	slacken	sling
sirup	slade	slink
sist	slag	slip
sister	slain	slipper
sisterhood	slake	slippery
sister-in-law	slam	slit
sisterly	slander	sliver
sit	slanderous	sloam
site	slang	sloat
sitology	slant	sloe
sitter	slap	sloop
sitting	slash	slop
situation	slat	slope
sixpence	slatch	sloping
sixpenny	slate	sloppy
sixteen	slaughter	slot
sixth	slaughter-house	sloth
sixty	slav	slothful
size	slave	slothful-ness
skate	slaver	slouch
skater	slavery	slough
skeleton	slavish	sloven
skelp	slavonic	slovenly
skep	slay	slow
skerry	sleave	slower
sketch	sled	slowly
shetchy	sledge	slue
skew	sleek	slug
skewer	sleep	sluggard
skid	sleeper	sluice
skies	sleepless	slum
skilful	sleepless-ness	slumber
skill	sleepy	slump
skim	sleet	slung
skin	sleeve	slur
skinny	sleigh	slut
skip	sleight	sly
skipper	slender	smack
skirmish		smacked

small	snip	softer
smallest	snivel	softly
smart	sniveller	soil
smartest	snob	soiled
smarting	snobbish-	soirée
smash	ness	sojourn
smatter	snooze	sol
smear	snore	solace
smeary	snort	solar
smell	snorting	solarize
smelt	snout	sold
smift	snow	solder
smile	snow-ball	soldier
smiled	snow-capt	sole
smiling	snowdrop	solecism
smirch	snowy	solemn
smirk	snub	solemnity
smite	snubbed	solemnize
smith	snuff	solicit
smitt	snug	solicitor
smitten	snuggled	solicitous
smock	so	solid
smoke	soak	solidly
smoker	soap	solidify
smoking	soapy	solidity
smoky	soar	solifidian
smooth	sob	soliloquy
smoothly	sober	solitaire
smoothness	sobriety	solitary
smote	sobriquet	solitude
smother	sociable	solo
smudge	sociably	solstice
smug	social	soluble
smuggle	socialism	solution
smuggler	socialist	solve
smut	society	solved
snack	sociology	solvent
snag	sock	some
snail	socket	somatic
snake	socle	sombre
snap	socratic	some
snap-shot	sod	somebody
snare	soda	somehow
snarl	sodality	someone
snatch	sodden	somersault
snathe	sodium	something
sneak	sofa	sometime
sneer	soffit	somewhat
sneeze	soft	somewhere
sniff	soften	somnambulate

*~ *idity may thus be expressed.* ** *os*

somnambu-	sounded	specious
list	sounding	speck
somnolence	soundless	speckle
son	soup	spectacle
song	sour	spectator
songster	source	spectral
soniferous	souse	spectre
son-in-law	south	specular
sonnet	southern	speculate
sonorous	souvenir	speculation
soon	sovereign	speculative
sooner	sow	speculator
soonest	sower	speech
soot	soy	speechless
sooth	spa	speed
soothe	space	speedy
soothing	spacious	spelk
soothsay	spade	spell
sop	spahi	spelling
sophist	spalt	spelt
sophister	span	spence
sophistical	spangle	spend
sophisti-cate	spaniel	spendthrift
sophistry	spanish	spent
soporific	spank	sperm-oil
soprano	spar	sphacelate
sorbate	spare	spheral*
sorcerer	spark	sphere
sorcery	sparkle	spheric
sordid	sparkling	sphinx
sore	sparrow	sphygmic
sorex	sparse	spicate
sorn	spasm	spice
sorrel	spasmodic	spicy
sorrow	spat	spider
sorrowful	spatter	spies
sorry	spawn	spike
sort	speak	spikenard
sortie	speaker	spiky
sortilege	spear	spill
sortment	special	spilt
sorts	specialised	spin
sot	specialist	spinach
sou	speciality	spinal
soubrette	specially	spindle
sough	specie	spine
sought	species	spinescent
soul	specific	spinet
sound	specify	spinner
	specimen	spinosity

* Preceding F, S may be expressed by E.

spinster	spouse	squire
spiral	spout	squirm
spire	sprain	squirrel
spirit	sprang	squirt
spirited	sprat	stab
spiritless	sprawl	stability
spiritual	spray	stable
spiritual-ism	spread	stableman
spiritualist	spreader	stack
spirituality	spree	stacte
spissitude	sprig	staddle-
spit	sprightly	stadium
spite	spring	staff
spiteful	springe	stag
spitfire	sprinkle	stage
splash	sprinkling	stager
splashed	sprite	stagger
splasher	sprout	stagnant
spleen	spruce	stagnation
splendent	sprung	stain
splendid	spry	stained
splendour	spumescence	stainless
splenetic	spur	stair
splice	spurge	staircase
splint	spurious	stair-way
splinter	spurn	stake
split	spurt	stalactite
splutter	sputter	stale
spoil	spy	stalemate
spoke	squab	stalk
spoken	squabble	stall
spoliate	squad	stallion
spoliation	squadron	stalwart
spondee	squalid	stamen
sponge	squall	stammer
spongy	squalor	stamp
sponsal	squama	stand
sponsor	square	standard
spontaneous	squash	standing
spoon	squashed	stand-point
sporadic	squat	stang
spore	squaw	stanhope
sporran	squeak	stannary
sport	squeal	stanza
sportive	squeamish	staphyle
sportsman	squeeze	staple
spot	squeezed	star
spotless	squib	starch
spotted	squill	starched
	squint	stare

stark	steam	stick
starless	steam-boat	stickle
starlight	steam-	sticky
starling	engine	stiff
starry	steamer	stiffen
start	steaming	stifle
started	steam-ship	stigma
startle	stearine	stigmatic
startling	steatoma	stile
starvation	steed	stilletto
starve	steel	still
stasis	steep	stimulant
statant	steeple	stimulate
state	steeple-	stimulation
stated	chase	stimulus
state-house	steer	sting
stately	steerage	stingy
statement	stela	stink
statesman	stellate	stint
statesman-	stem	stipend
like	stemple	stipple
statesman-	stench	stipulate
ship	stencil	stipulation
statesmen	stenograph	stir
static	stenogra-	stirrup
station	pher	stitch
stationary	stenography	stoat
stationer	stentorian	stock
stationery	step	stockade
statist	step-mother	stock-
statistics	stere	exchange
statue	stereograph	stocking
statuette	stereoscope	stoic
stature	stereotype	stoical
statute	sterile	stoicism
staunch	sterility	stoke
stave	sterilize	stoker
stay	sterling	stole
stayed	stern	stolen
stead	sternum	stolid
steadfast	stet	stoma
steadfast-	stethometer	stomach
ness	stew	stomatitis
steadily	steward	stone
steadiness	steward-	stood
steady	ship	stool
steak	stewed	stoom
steal	stiacciato	stoop
stealth	stich	stop
stealthy	stichic	stoppage

storage	stretch	stuffy
store	stretcher	stultify
stored	strew	stultiloquy
storm	striate	stum
stormy	strict	stumble
story	strictest	stumbling
stout	strictly	stumbling-
stove	stricture	block
stow	stride	stump
strabism	strife	stun
straddle	strike	stung
straggle	striker	stunt
straggler	string	stunted
straggling	stringent	stupa
straight	strip	stupe
straight-	stripe	stupefac-
forward	stripling	tion
strain	strive	stupefy
strait	striven	stupendous
straiten	strix	stupid
strand	strode	stupidity
stranded	stroke	stupor
strange	stroll	sturdier
stranger	stroma	sturdy
strangle	strong	stutter
strangler	stronger	sty
strangu-	stronghold	style
lation	strongly	stylish
strap	strop	stylography
strass	struck	styptic
strata	structure	styx
stratagem	struggle	suasion
strategy	struggling	suave
strath	strum	suavity
stratum	strut	subaction
stratus	strychnine	subaltern
straw	stub	subaquatic
strawberry	stubble	subconscious
stray	stubborn	sub-contract
streak	stubborn-	subdivision
stream	ness	subdominant
streamer	stucco	subdue
streaming	stuck	subdued
street	stud	sud-editor
strength	student	suberic
strengthen	studied	suberous
strength-	studio	subgenus
ener	studious	subjacent
strenuous	study	subject
stress	stuff	subjection

subjugate
subjunctive
sublate
sublet
subligation
sublime
sublimity
subliticn
submarine
submerge
submission
submissive
submit
submitted
subnascent
subordinate
subordina-
    tion
suborn
subreption
subrogation
subscribe
subscript
subscription
subsection
subsequent
subsequently
subserve
subser-
    vient
subside
subsided
subsidy
subsist
substance
substantial
substantive
substitutes
substruction
substyle
subsumption
subtend
subterete
subterfuge
subterran-
    ean
subtile
subtle
subtlety
subtract

suburbs
suburban
subvention
subvert
subway
succeed
success
successful
succession
successive
successor
succiduous
succinct
succory
succotash
succour
succula
succulent
succumb
succussion
such
suck
sucker
suckling
suction
sudation
sudden
suddenly
sue
sued
suet
suffer
sufferable
sufferance
sufferer
suffering
suffice
sufficed
sufficient
suffix
suffocate
suffocation
suffrage
suffragette
suffumigate
sugar
sugary
sugescent
suggest
suggestion

suggestive
suggilation
suicidal
suicide
suit
suitable
suite
suitor
sulk
sulky
sullen
sully
sulphate
sulphur
sulphurate
sulphurous
sultan
sultry
sum
summarily
summary
summer
summit
summon
summoned
summons
sump
sumptuous
sumptuously
sun
sunday
sunder
sundown
sundry
sung
sunk
sunken
sun-light
sunlit
sunny
sunrise
sunset
sunshine
sup
superable
superabun-
    dance
superabun-
    dant
superannuate

superb	supplication	surveillance
supercilious	supply	survey
supercil-	support	surveyor
iously	supportable	survival
superem-	supported	survive
inent	supporter	survivor
superexcel-	supports	susceptible
lence	suppose	suscipient
superficial	supposition	suspect
superfluous	suppress	suspected
superhuman	suppressed	suspend
superintend	suppression	suspense
superinten-	suppurate	suspension
dence	suppuration	suspicious
superintendent	supputation	suspiral
superior	supremacy	sustain
superiority	supreme	sustenance
superlative	surbase	sutler
supermun-	surbate	suttle
dane	surbed	suture
supernacular	surcease	swab
supernatant	surcharge	swaddle
supernat-	surd	swag
ural	sure	swage
supernu-	surely	swain
merary	sureness	swale
superpose	surest	swallow
superroyal	surety	swam
supersalient	surf	swamp
superscribe	surface	swampy
superscrip-	surfeit	swan
tion	surge	sward
supersede	surgeon	swarm
supersedure	surgery	swarthy
superstition	surgical	swash
superstitious	surly	swathe
superstruct	surmise	sway
supervene	surmount	swear
supervise	surmounted	sweat
supervision	surname	sweep
supination	surpass	sweeper
supine	surplice	sweet
supper	surplus	sweet-bread
supplant	surprise	sweeten
supple	surprising	sweeter
supplement	surrender	swell
supple-	surreptitious	swelter
mentary	surrogate	swift
suppliant	surround	swiftly
supplicate	surroundings	swiftness

swim	synoptical	taintless
swindle	synovia	take
swindled	syntax	taken
swindler	synteretic	talbot
swindling	synthesis	talc
swine	syringe	tale
swing	syrup	tale-bearer
swirl	system	talent
swiss	systematic	tales
switch	systemati-	talion
switchback	cally	talisman
swivel	systematist	talk
swollen	systematize	talkative
swoon	systole	talker
swoop	systyle	talking
sword	syzygy	tall
swore		tallow
sworn	Tab	tally
sycamore	tabard	talus
sycophant	tabby	tamable
sycosis	tabernacle	tamarind
syllable	tabes	tambour
syllabus	tabid	tamboureen
syllepsis	tablature	tame
syllogism	table	tameless
sylph	tableau	tamer
sylva	table-land	tamis
sylvan	tablet	tamp
symbol	taboo	tamper
symbolic	tabour	tan
symbolism	tabular	tandem
symmet-	tabulate	tang
rical	tace	tangent
symmetry	tache	tangible
sympathetic	tachyg-	tangle
sympathy	raphy	tank
symphony	tacit	tankard
symphysis	tacitly	tanner
symptom	taciturn	tannery
symptosia	tack	tantalize
synagogue	tackle	tantalized
syncope	tact	tantalizing
syndicate	tactics	tantalus
synepy	taction	tap
synergy	tactless	tape
syngraph	taffeta	taper
synod	tag	tapestry
synonym	tail	tapioca
synonymous	tailor	tapis
synopsis	taint	tapster

+ Exception; to distinguish from energy ....

tar	tearful	tenacious
tardy	tease	tenacity
tare	teasel	tenancy
target	tea-spoon	tenant
tariff	teat	tenantable
tarn	teathe	tend
tarnish	technic	tendency
tarpauling	technique	tender
tarrace	technology	tenderly
tarry	tedious	tenderness
tart	tedium	tendon
tartan	teem	tendril
tartar	teeming	tenebrous
tartarus	teen	tenement
task	teeth	tenet
tasse	teetotal	tenfold
tassel	teetotaler	tennis
taste	teetotum	tenon
tasteful	tegument	tenor
tasteless	telary	tense
taster	telegram	tension
tasty	telegraph	tensity
tatter	telegraphic	tent
tattered	telegraphy	tentacle
tattle	teleology	tenter
tattler	telephone	tenth
tattoo	telescope	tenure
tau	telic	tepefy
taught	tell	tepid
taunt	temerity	teratology
taurine	temper	terce
taurus	temperament	tercel
tautulogy	temperance	tercen-
tavern	temperate	tenary
taw	tempra-	terebrate
tawdry	ture	term
tawny	tempests	termagant
tawse	tempestuous	terminal
tax	templar	terminate
taxable	temple	termination
taxation	temporal	terminist
taxidermy	temporary	terminology
taxus	temporize	terminus
tea	tempt	tern
teach	temptation	ternary
teacher	tempter	terrace
teak	temulent	terrel
teal	ten	terrestrial
team	tenable	terrible
tear	tenace	terrier

terrific	themselves	thistle
terrify	then	thither
territory	thence	thole
terror	theocracy	tholobate
terrorism	theologian	thong
terse	theology	thor
tertiate	theopathy	thoral
tessellated	theorem	thorax
test	theoretical	thorn
testaceous	theory	thorough
testament	theosophist	thorough-
testate	theosophy	bred
testator	thera-	thorough-
tester	peutic	fare
testicle	there	thoroughly
testify	thereabout	thorp
testimonial	thereafter	those
testimony	thereat	thou
testy	thereby	though
tete	therefore	thought
tether	therein	thoughtful
tetragon	thereon	thoughtless
tetrarch	thermal	thousand
teuton	thermom-	thraldom
teutonic	eter	thrash
tew	thermoscope	thread
text	thermotic	threadbare
textile	these	threat
texture	thesis	threaten
thalia	theurgy	three
than	thew	threnetic
thane	they	threnody
thank	thick	threshold
thankful	thicken	threw
thankfulness	thief	thrift
thank-	thieve	thrifty
offering	thigh	thrill
thanksgiving	thill	thrive
tharm	thimble	throat
that	thin	throb
thatch	thine	throe
thaw	thing	throne
the	think	throng
theatre	thinker	throttle
theatrical	third	through
theft	thirst	throughout
their	thirsty	throw
theism	thirteen	thrown
them	thirty	thrum
theme	this	thrush

thrust	timbre	tobacco-
thud	time	nist
thumb	timeous	tobine
thummim	timid	tobit
thump	timidity	tobogan
thunder	tin	tocher
thunder-	tincture	tocology
bolt	tinder	tod
thunderous	tine	to-day
thurible	tinge	toddle
thurls	tingle	toddy
thursday	tingling	toe
thus	tiniest	toffee
thwaite	tinkle	toft
thwart	tinsel	toga
thy	tint	together
thyme	tintamar	toggle
thymus	tintinnab-	toil
thyself	ulation	toiler
tiara	tiny	toilet
tibia	tip	tokay
tibial	tippet	token
tick	tipple	tola
ticket	tippler	toledo
tickle	tipsy	tolerable
tickler	tir	tolerance
ticklish	tirade	tolerant
tidal	tire	tolerate
tide	tiredness	toleration
tidied	tiresome	toll
tidings	tissue	toller
tidology	tit	toll-gate
tidy	titanic	tolsey
tie	tithes	tomahawk
tied	titillation	tomato
tier	title	tomb
tierce	titmouse	tombed
tiff	titration	tome
tiffany	titter	tomentum
tig	titular	tomin
tiger	tiver	to-morrow
tight	tmesis	tomtit
tightly	to	tomtom
tightness	toad	ton
tile	toady	tone
till	toast	toned
tiller	toasted	toneless
tiller-rope	toaster	tong
tilt	toastmaster	tongue
timber	tobacco	tonic

to-night	tossing	traduce
tonnage	tost	traffic
tonsil	tot	tragedy
tonsilitis	total	tragical
tonsure	totter	trail
tontine	tottery	train
tool	touch	trainer
toot	touching	train-oil
tooter	touchy	trait
tooth	tough	traitorous
tooth-ache	tour	traitors
top	tourist	traitress
topaz	tourn	traject
tope	tournament	tralation
tophet	tournure	tram
topic	touse	trammel
topical	tout	tramp
top-mast	tow	trample
topography	towage	tramway
topple	toward	trance
toque	towards	tranquil
torah	towel	tranquil-
torch	tower	lize
torch-light	town	tranquillity
tore	township	transact
torment	toxical	transactions
tormentor	toxicology	trans-
tormina	toy	atlantic
tornado	trabeation	transcend
torpedo	trace	transcendent
torpent	traceable	transcribe
torpid	tracery	transcrip-
torpor	trachea	tion
torque	tracheal	transept
torrefy	tracheotomy	transfer
torrent	trachoma	transferable
torrential	tracing	transfig-
torrid	track	uration
torse	tract	transfigure
torsel	tractable	transfix
torsion	tractarian	transform
torso	traction	transfor-
tort	tractive	mation
tortive	tractor	transfuse
tortulous	trade	transgress
tortuous	trader	transgression
torture	tradespeople	transgres-
torus	trade-wind	sor
tory	tradition	transient
toss	traditional	transire

transit	trave	triblet
transition	travel	tribulation
transitive	traveller	tribune
translate	travelling	tributary
translation	travesty	tribute
translit-	trawl	trick
erate	trawler	trickle
translucent	tray	tricolour
transmi-	treacherous	tricycle
grant	treachery	tride
transmigrate	treacle	trident
transmi-	tread	triennial
gration	treadle	trifles
transmis-	treason	trifling
sible	treasonable	trig
transmission	treasure	trigamist
transmit	treasurer	trigamous
transmittal	treasury	trigamy
transmutable	treat	trigger
transmute	treatise	triglyph
transom	treatment	trigon
transparency	treaty	trigraph
transparent	treble	trilingual
transpicuous	tred	triliteral
transpiration	tree	trill
transpire	trefoil	trillion
transplant	trellis	trilogy
transplen-	tremble	trim
dent	trembling	trimeter
transport	tremendous	trimetric
transpor-	tremor	trine
tation	tremulous	trinity
transposal	trench	trinket
transpose	trenchant	trio
transubstan-	trend	trior
tiation	trendle	trip
transude	trepan	tripe
transumpt	trespass	tripthong
transverse	trespasser	triple
trap	tress	triplet
trapa	trestles	tripod
trapan	tret	tripos
trap-door	trey	tripper
trapeze	triable	tripsis
trapper	triad	triptych
trappist	trial	trireme
trash	triangle	trisect
trass	triarchy	trismus
traumatic	tribal	trispaston
travail	tribe	trisyllable

trite	trump	turban
tritheism	trumpet	turbid
triton	truncate	turbinate
triumph	truncheon	turbine
triumphal	trundle	turbit
triumphant	truss	turbot
triune	trust	turbulent
trivet	trustee	tureen
trivial	trustful	turf
trivium	trustworthy	turgent
troat	trusty	turgescent
trochaic	truth	turgid
troche	truthful	turkey
trochee	truthfulness	turkish
trod	try	turn
trogon	tryst	turn-coat
trojan	tub	turned
troll	tube	turner
trombone	tubercle	turnery
tromp	tuberculate	turnip
troop	tubercu-	turnkey
trope	losis	turnover
trophi	tuberous	turnpike
trophy	tubular	turnspit
tropical	tuck	turnstile
tropics	tudor	turpentine
tropology	tuesday	turpitude
trot	tuff	turquois
troth	tuft	turret
trouble	tug	turtle
troublesome	tugger	turtle-dove
troublous	tuition	tusk
trough	tulip	tussle
troupe	tulle	tutelage
trousers	tumble	tutor
trousseau	tumbler	tutorial
trout	tumbrel	tuyere
trover	tumid	twaddle
trow	tumour	twain
trowel	tumult	twang
truant	tumultuous	tweak
truce	tun	tweeds
trucidation	tundra	twelfth
truck	tune	twelve
truckle	tuned	twenty
truculent	tuner	twice
trudge	tunic	twig
true	tunnel	twilight
truffle	tup	twill
truism	turanian	twin

twine	umbel	unattainable
twinge	umber	unattended
twinkle	umbilical	unavailable
twirl	umbo	unavenged
twist	umbra	unavoidable
twisted	umbrage	unaware
twister	umbratic	unbar
twit	umbrella	unbearable
twitch	umpire	unbecoming
twitter	unabashed	unbegotten
two	unabated	unbelief
two-fold	unable	unbeliever
tympan	unabsolved	unbend
tympanum	unabsorbed	unbias
type	unaccented	unbidden
typewriting	unaccep-	unblemished
typhoid	table	unblest
typhoon	unaccomodated	unblushing
typhus	unaccom-	unbolt
typical	panied	unbosom
typify	unaccount-	unbounded
typography	able	unbuckle
typology	unaccus-	unbuilt
tyrannical	tomed	unburden
tyrannous	unacknow-	uncalled
tyranny	ledged	uncase
tyrant	unacquainted	uncaught
tyro	unaddicted	unceasing
	unadorned	uncensured
Uberty	unadvisable	uncertainty
ubiquity	unaffected	unchallenged
udder	unaided	unchanged
ugliest	unalloyed	uncharitable
ugly	unanimity	unchartered
uhlan	unanimous	unchaste
ukase	unannounced	uncheered
ulcer	unanswer-	unchival-
ulcerate	able	rous
ule	unappreciated	unchristian
ulex	unapproach-	uncircum-
ullage	able	cised
ulmic	unappro-	uncivil
ulna	priated	uncivilized
ulster	unarm	unclad
ulterior	unashamed	unclaimed
ultimate	unasked	unclasp
ultimately	unaspiring	uncle
ultimatum	unassigned	unclean
ultramun-	unassuming	unclipped
dane	unattached	unclose

unclothe	underbred	undressed
uncoil	undercurrent	undue
uncoloured	underfeed	undulate
uncombed	underfoot	unduly
uncomfort-able	undergo	unduteous
	undergone	undutiful
uncomforted	undergrad-uate	undying
uncommon		unearned
uncommuni-cated	underground	unearthly
	underhand	uneasy
uncompass-ionate	underived	uneatable
	underlay	uneducated
uncomplain-ing	undermine	unembar-rassed
	underneath	
uncomplai-sant	underpay	unembodied
	underpin	unemployed
uncompressed	underrate	unending
unconceived	undersell	unendowed
unconcern	understand	unendurable
uncondemned	understanding	unengaged
uncondi-tional	understood	unenlight-ened
	undertake	
unconfessed	undervalue	unenvied
unconfirmed	undeserved	unequal
unconfused	undesigned	unequivocal
unconquer-able	undetected	unerring
	undeveloped	unessential
unconscion-able	undid	uneven
	undigested	unexamined
unconscious	undimin-ished	unexampled
unconstrained		unexecuted
unconsumed	undine	unexercised
uncontested	undinted	unexpected
uncontrolled	undiscerned	unexposed
uncouth	undisci-plined	unexpressed
uncover		unextended
unction	undiscovered	unfading
unctuous	undisguised	unfailingly
uncut	undismayed	unfair
undamaged	undisputed	unfaithful
undated	undistin-guished	unfaltering
undaunted		unfamiliar
undeceive	undisturbed	unfashion-able
undecided	undivided	
undefended	undo	unfathomed
undefiled	undomesti-cated	unfavourable
undefinable		unfed
undemon-strative	undone	unfeeling
	undoubtedly	unfeigned
under	undreamed	unfelt

unfetter
unfit
unfix
unflinching
unfold
unforeseen
unforgiven
unformed
unfortunate
unfounded
unfriendly
unfrock
unfruitful
unfurnish
ungainly
ungallant
ungodly
ungovernable
ungraceful
ungracious
ungrammat-
    ical
ungranted
ungratified
unguarded
unguent
unguical
ungulate
unhallow
unhappy
unharness
unhealthy
unheeded
unhesitating
unhinge
unholy
unhorse
unicorn
unideal
unifacial
uniform
uniformity
unigenous
unimaginable
unimpaired
unimpeded
unimportant
unimposing
unindorsed
uninfluenced

uninformed
uninhabited
uninjured
uninspired
unintellec-
    tual
uninten-
    tionally
uninterested
uninterrupted
uninvited
union
unionist
unique
unison
unit
unitarian
unite
united
unity
universal
universally
universe
university
univocal
unjust
unkempt
unkind
unknown
unladen
unlamented
unlawful
unleavened
unless
unlighted
unlike
unlikely
unlimited
unlock
unloose
unlovely
unloving
unlucky
unmade
unmake
unman
unmanage-
    able
unmanly
unmarried

unmasked
unmeaning
unmentioned
unmerciful
unmindful
unmistaken
unmitigated
unmixed
unmoved
unmusical
unnatural
unnavigable
unnecessary
unnerve
unnoted
unobservant
unofficial
unopened
unopposed
unpacked
unpaid
unpalatable
unpardon-
    able
unpaved
unperturbed
unpleasant
unpractical
unprece-
    dented
unprejudiced
unprepared
unpretend-
    ing
unprincipled
unprinted
unproclaimed
unproductive
unprofitable
unpromising
unpronounced
unpropitious
unproved
unprovided
unprovoked
unpublished
unpunished
unqualified
unquenched
unquiet

unravel	unskilled	untruth
unreadable	unsociable	untwist
unready	unsold	unused
unreal	unsolid	unusual
unreason-	unsound	unutterable
able	unsown	unvalued
unreconciled	unspeakable	unveil
unrecovered	unspecified	unversed
unredeemed	unspoiled	unwarlike
unrefined	unspotted	unwarrant-
unrefreshed	unstained	able
unreliable	unsteady	unwary
unremuner-	unstinted	unwelcome
ative	unsubdued	unwell
unrenowned	unsuccessful	unwholesome
unresented	unsuitable	unwifely
unreserve	unsuited	unwilling
unreser-	unsurpass-	unwind
vedly	able	unwise
unrespited	unsuspected	unwittingly
unrest	unsuspicious	unwonted
unrestrained	unsustain-	unworthy
unrighteous	able	unwritten
unripe	unswayed	unyoke
unromantic	unswerving	up
unruffle	unsystematic	upbraid
unruled	untainted	upbringing
unruly	untamed	upheaval
unsafe	untasted	upheld
unsaid	untaxed	uphill
unsated	untenable	uphold
unsatisfactory	untenanted	upholster
unsatisfied	untested	upland
unsavoury	unthankful	uplift
unsay	untidy	upon
unscattered	untie	upper
unscrew	until	uppermost
unscrupulous	untimely	upright
unseal	untiring	uproar
unsearchable	unto	upset
unseasonable	untold	upside down
unseemly	untouched	upstairs
unseen	untoward	uranus
unselfish	untraced	urban
unsettled	untractable	urbanity
unsex	untrained	urchin
unshaken	untried	urge
unsheathe	untrod	urgent
unshod	untroubled	urn
unsightly	untrue	us

usage	valuation	velvet
usance	value	venal
use	valuer	venation
used	valve	vend
useful	vamp	vendetta
usher	vampire	veneer
ustion	vamps	venerable
usual	van	venerate
usually	vandal	venereal
usurer	vane	venetian
usurp	van-guard	vengeance
utensil	vanish	venial
utilitarian	vanity	venison
utility	vanquish	venom
utilize	vantage	venomous
utmost	vapid	venous
utopia	vaporific	vent
utter	vapour	ventilate
utterance	variable	ventilation
utterly	variance	ventriil-
uttermost	variation	oquism
uvula	varicous	venture
uxorious	varied	venturesome
	varies	venturous
	variety	venus
Vacancy	various	veracious
vacant	varlet	veranda
vacate	varnish	verb
vacation	vary	verbal
vaccinate	vascular	verbatim
vaccine	vase	verbena
vacillate	vaseline	verbose
vacuous	vassal	verdant
vacuum	vast	verdict
vagabond	vat	verdigris
vagina	vatican	verdure
vagrant	vaudeville	verge
vague	vault	verger
vaguely	vaunt	verification
vain	veal	verify
valance	veer	vermicelli
vale	vegetable	vermicide
valentine	vegetarian	vermiculate
valet	vehement	vermifuge
valiant	vehicle	vermilion
valid	veil	vermin
validity	vein	verminate
valise	vell	vernacular
valley	vellum	vernal
valour	velocity	vernant
valuable		

vernility	vicarage	violent
verrucose	vicarious	violet
versable	vice	violin
versant	vicegerent	violinist
versatile	vice-	violincello
versatility	president	viper
verse	viceroy	virago
versed	vice versa	virent
verser	vicinity	virgin
version	vicious	virginity
versus	victim	virgo
vert	victor	virile
vertebra	victoria	virtual
vertex.	victorious	virtue
vertical	victory	virtuosity
verticity	victual	virtuous
vertigo	vie	virulence
verve	view	virulent
very	viewpoint	virus
vesical	vigil	vis
vesicle	vigilance	visage
vesper	vigilant	viscera
vessel	vignette	viscid
vest	vigorous	viscount
vesta	vigorously	viscous
vestal	vigour	visé
vested	viking	visible
vestibule	vile	vision
vestige	villa	visionary
vestment	village	visit
vestry	villain	visitant
vesture	villainous	visitation
vetch	villainy	visitor
veteran	vincible	visor
veterinary	vindicable	vista
veto	vindicate	visual
vetust	vindication	vital
vex	vindicative	vitality
vexation	vindicator	vitiate
vexatious	vine	vitilitigate
vexed	vinegar	vitriol
via	vinery	vituperate
viable	vineyard	vivacious
viaduct	vintage	vivacity
vial	viol	vivid
viand	viola	vividly
viaticum	violable	vivisection
vibrate	violate	vixen
vibration	violation	vizier
vicar	violence	vocabulary

vocal	Wabble	war
vocalist	wad	warble
vocaliza-tion	wadding	warbling
	waddle	ward
vocation	wade	warden
vocative	wading	warder
vociferate	wafer	wardrobe
vociferous	waft	wardship
vogue	wag	ware
voice	wage	warehouse
void	wager	warfare
voidance	wages	warlike
volatile	wagon	warm
volcanic	wagoner	warmer
volcano	wagtail	warmth
vole	waif	warn
volition	wail	warning
volley	wain	war-office
volt	wainscot	warp
voluble	waist	warrant
volume	waistband	warrantable
voluminous	waistcoat	warren
voluntary	wait	warrior
volunteer	waiter	war-ship
voluptuous	waitress	wart
vomit	waits	wary
vomited	waive	was
voracious	waiver	wase
voracity	wake	wash
vortex	wakefulness	washable
votary	waken	wasp
vote	wale	wassail
voter	walk	wast
votive	wall	waste
vouch	wallet	wasted
voucher	wallow	wasteful
vouchsafe	walnut	wastrel
vow	walrus	watch
vowel	waltz	watchfulness
voyage	waltzed	watch-maker
voyager	wampum	watchman
vulcan	wan	water
vulcanite	wand	water-cart
vulgar	wander	water-colour
vulgarity	wandering	water-cress
vulgate	wane	watered
vulnerable	want	water-fall
vulnerate	wanton	water-fowl
vulture	wantonly	water-hen
vying	wantonness	water-pot

waterproof
water-tight
watery
wattle
wave
waver
wavering
wavy
wax
waxen
waxy
way
wayfarer
waylay
wayside
wayward
we
weak
weakly
weakness
weal
weald
wealth
wealthiest
wealthy
wean
weapon
wear
wearable
weariness
wearisome
weary
weasel
weather
weather-
   cock
weave
weaver
web
wed
wedding
wedge
wedlock
wednesday
wee
weed
week
weekly
ween
weep

weigh
weight
weighty
weir
weird
weirdest
welcome
weld
welfare
welkin
well
well-known
well-nigh
welsh
welt
wench
wend
went
were
wert
wesleyan
west
western
westward
wet
wey
whack
whale
whalebone
whaler
wharf
wharves
what
whatsoever
wheal
wheat
wheedle
wheel
wheel-barrow
wheels
wheeze
whelk
whelm
whelp
when
whence
whenever
where
whereabout
whereas

whereat
whereby
wherefore
wherein
wheresoever
wherever
wherry
whet
whether
whetstone
whey
which
whichsoever
whiff
whig
while
whilst
whim
whimsical
whin
whine
whip
whir
whirl
whirling
whirlpool
whirlwind
whisk
whisker
whiskey
whisper
whist
whistle
whit
white
whiten
whitewash
whither
whiting
whitlow
whitsuntide
whittle
whiz
who
whoever
whole
wholesale
wholesome
wholly
whom

whoop	winter	womanhood
whore	winze	womanly
whorl	wipe	womb
whort	wiped	women
whose	wiper	won
whosoever	wire	wonder
why	wireless	wonderful
wick	wiry	wonderland
wicked	wisdom	wondrous
wicker	wise	wont
wicket	wiser	wonted
wide	wisest	woo
widen	wish	wood
widely	wished	wood-cut
widow	wisp	wooded
widower	wist	wooden
width	wistful	woodland
wield	wit	woodpecker
wife	witch	woody
wifely	witchcraft	woof
wig	with	wool
wight	withal	woold
wigwam	withdraw	woollen
wild	withdrawal	woolly
wilderness	withdrawn	word
wile	wither	worded
wilful	withered	wording
will	withold	wordy
willing	within	wore
willow	without	work
wily	withstand	workable
wimble	withstood	worker
wimple	witless	work-house
win	witling	workman
wince	witness	workmanship
wind(n)	witnessed	workshop
wind(v)	witnessing	world
windfall	witticism	worldly
windle	witty	world-wide
window	wives	worm
windpipe	wizard	worming
windward	wizen	worn
windy	woad	worried
wine	woe	worry
wing	woeful	worse
wingless	woes	worship
wink	wold	worst
winner	wolf	wort
winnow	wolves	worth
winsome	woman	worthless

worthy	xenodochy	young
wot	xenophon	younger
would	xerasia	youngest
wound	xerodes	your
wounded	xylanthrax	yours
wove	xylography	yourself
woven	xyloid	youth
wrack	xylol	youths
wraith	xyst	yule
wrangle	xyster	
wrangler		Zambo
wrap	Yacht	zany
wrapper	yager	zapote
wrath	yak	zareba
wreak	yam	zeal
wreath	yama	zealot
wreck	yank	zealous
wren	yankee	zebra
wrench	yap	zenana
wrenched	yard	zenith
wrest	yare	zephyr
wrested	yarn	zero
wrestle	yarrow	zest
wrestler	yawl	zeta
wretch	yawn	zeus
wretched	ye	zigzag
wriggle	yea	zinc
wright	year	zincke
wring	yearly	zincode
wrinkle	yearn	zincography
wrist	yeast	zion
writ	yell	zoanthropy
write / or /	yellow	zodiac
writer	yelp	zonate
writhe	yeoman	zone
written	yeomanry	zoo
wrong	yerk	zoogeny
wrongfully	yes	zoography
wrote	yesterday	zoological
wroth	yet	zoology
wrought	yew	zoonomy
wry	yield	zoophyte
	yielding	zootomist
Xangti	yoga	zopissa
xanthein	yoke	zouave
xanthidium	yokel	zulu
xanthine	yolk	zymology
xanthocon	yonder	zymometer
xantippe	yore	zymosis
xebic	you	zythum

Lightning Source UK Ltd.
Milton Keynes UK
UKHW022220010223
416324UK00005B/92